MAX notes

Richard Wright's

Native Son

Text by
Richard Bucci
(B.A., University of California at Berkeley)
Consulting Editor
University of California at Berkeley
Berkeley, California

Illustrations by
Arnold Turovskiy

Research & Education Association

MAXnotes® for
NATIVE SON

Printed in the United States of America

Library of Congress Catalog Card Number 96-67428

International Standard Book Number 0-87891-035-2

MAXnotes® is a registered trademark of
Research & Education Association, Piscataway, New Jersey 08854

What **MAXnotes**® *Will Do for You*

This book is intended to help you absorb the essential contents and features of Richard Wright's *Native Son* and to help you gain a thorough understanding of the work. The book has been designed to do this more quickly and effectively than any other study guide.

For best results, this **MAXnotes** book should be used as a companion to the actual work, not instead of it. The interaction between the two will greatly benefit you.

To help you in your studies, this book presents the most up-to-date interpretations of every section of the actual work, followed by questions and fully explained answers that will enable you to analyze the material critically. The questions also will help you to test your understanding of the work and will prepare you for discussions and exams.

Meaningful illustrations are included to further enhance your understanding and enjoyment of the literary work. The illustrations are designed to place you into the mood and spirit of the work's settings.

The **MAXnotes** also include summaries, character lists, explanations of plot, and section-by-section analyses. A biography of the author and discussion of the work's historical context will help you put this literary piece into the proper perspective of what is taking place.

The use of this study guide will save you the hours of preparation time that would ordinarily be required to arrive at a complete grasp of this work of literature. You will be well prepared for classroom discussions, homework, and exams. The guidelines that are included for writing papers and reports on various topics will prepare you for any added work which may be assigned.

The **MAXnotes** will take your grades "to the max."

Dr. Max Fogiel
Program Director

Contents

Section One: *Introduction* 1

  The Life and Work of Richard Wright.................... 1

  Historical Background 6

  Master List of Characters....................................... 7

  Summary of the Novel 8

  Estimated Reading Time....................................... 10

Each Book includes List of Characters, Summary, Analysis, Study Questions and Answers, and Suggested Essay Topics.

Section Two: *Native Son* 12

  Book 1: Fear 12

  Book 2: Flight... 32

  Book 3: Fate 48

Section Three: *How "Bigger" Was Born* 66

Section Four: *Sample Analytical Paper Topics* 79

Section Five: *Bibliography* 85

Introduction

The Life and Work of Richard Wright

Richard Nathaniel Wright was born on September 4, 1908, in Roxie, Mississippi. He was a grandson of slaves. His father was an illiterate sharecropper, and his mother was a schoolteacher. When he was five, Wright's family moved to Tennessee, but his father soon deserted them, and from the age of ten, Wright had to interrupt his schooling to earn money. The family was not only faced with extreme poverty, but also with terrifying racial violence. When Richard was living with his aunt and uncle in Arkansas, his uncle was murdered by a white mob. Despite all the hardships he faced as a child, however, Richard managed to excel in school. By the time he completed the ninth grade, books were his constant companions.

Although Wright would leave the South forever when he was only nineteen, it is not surprising that his early life there made the deepest impressions on his personality, and supplied him with much of the subject matter for his later writings. What is remarkable, however, is that Wright accomplished his own transformation into a literary person there, while yet a teenager, and against almost impossible odds. He was poor, black and only semi-educated, and, most forbiddingly, he was subject to constant and often potentially deadly racist harassment. Readers can learn about the depth of his transformation, and the obstacles he faced while achieving it, from Wright's own compelling testimony in *Black Boy*, his autobiography. Wright described one defining moment of his self-education in especially vivid terms. When he was eighteen and working for an eyeglass company in Memphis, Tennessee, he read a story in a newspaper which attacked the writer H.L. Mencken. He became curious about why a white-owned newspaper would attack a prominent white writer, and decided that he must read Mencken's own writings. He had no money to buy books, and as an African American, he was forbidden to borrow books from the library. Wright took a risk and asked a fellow white employee—an Irish Catholic who was therefore also subject to the prejudices of other whites—if he could use his library card, and pretend he was borrowing books for him. The man agreed, and Richard Wright at last had his encounter with H.L. Mencken's *A Book of Prefaces*:

> That night in my rented room...I opened *A Book of Prefaces* and began to read. I was jarred and shocked by the style, the clear, clean, sweeping sentences. Why did he write like that? And how did one write like that? I pictured the man as a raging demon, slashing with his pen, consumed with hate, denouncing everything American, extolling everything European or German, laughing at the weaknesses of people, mocking God, authority. What was this? I stood up, trying to realize what reality lay behind the meaning of the words...Yes, this man was fighting, fighting with words. He was using words as a weapon, using them as one would use a club. Could words be weapons? Well, yes, for here they were. Then, maybe, perhaps, I could use them as a weapon? No. It frightened me. I read on and what amazed me was not what he said, but how on earth anybody had the courage to say it.
>
> Occasionally I glanced up to reassure myself that I was alone in the room. Who were these men about whom Mencken was talking so passionately? Who was Anatole France? Joseph Conrad? Sinclair Lewis, Sherwood Anderson, Dostoevski, George Moore, Gustave Flaubert, Maupassant, Tolstoy, Frank Harris, Mark Twain, Thomas Hardy, Arnold Bennett, Stephen Crane, Zola, Norris, Gorky, Bergson, Ibsen, Balzac, Bernard Shaw, Dumas, Poe, Thomas Mann, O. Henry, Dreiser, H. G. Wells, Gogol, T. S. Eliot, Gide, Baudelaire, Edgar Lee Masters, Stendahl, Turgenev, Huneker, Nietzsche, and scores of others? Were these men real? Did they exist or had they existed? And how did one pronounce their names? (*Black Boy*, p. 293)

Before too long, and with the help of his borrowed library card, Richard Wright filled in as many of the blank spaces in his learning as he could, absorbing book after book, like a starving man put before a Thanksgiving table.

In 1927, when he was nineteen, he and his aunt joined the great African-American migration to the North, settling in Chicago's vast South Side ghetto. Initially, Wright was in awe of his new surroundings, but he was already watchful, and concerned about the plight of African Americans, and poor people generally. Although he found racism everywhere in segregated Chicago, it was neither as profound nor as potentially deadly as it was in the South. Blacks and whites mingled in railway stations, streetcars, and downtown restaurants. The poor neighborhoods, black and white, seethed with subversive political activism, something Wright had never seen in the South. At first he was attracted to the black nationalist movement led by Marcus Garvey, but he eventually rejected Garvey's political philosophy as too narrow. Instead, Wright began his long involvement with communism, both because he felt the communists were more active than the nationalists in the day-to-day struggles of African Americans, and because the stated aim of communism was to break down the walls between black and white workers and build a new society free of all forms of oppression. In 1932, while working in the Chicago post office, some of his white co-workers invited Wright to a meeting of the John Reed Club. John Reed was an American writer who participated in the 1917 socialist revolution in Russia, and the American Communist Party set up literary clubs in his name across the country. Wright sooned joined both the John Reed Club and the Communist Party, and he began to contribute political poems and essays to such left-wing periodicals as *Anvil, Left Front,* and *The New Masses.* He also honed his skills by participating in the Federal Writers' Project of the Works Project Administration (WPA), a depression-era government program designed to provide work for the nation's millions of unemployed.

Wright thus simultaneously launched a literary and a political life in Chicago at the dawn of the 1930s—the decade of the Great Depression. By 1937, he was encouraged enough by his own writing talent to risk relocation to New York, the nation's literary capital.

There he soon became the Harlem correspondent for the *Daily Worker*, the Communist Party newspaper, and he also resumed publishing a series of five powerful stories about the South, which he had mainly written in Chicago. One of these stories, "Fire and Cloud," won an important prize as the best fiction written by a WPA writer. The prestigious award brought Wright to the attention of the New York literary establishment. In 1938—less than one year after he had left Chicago—Harper & Brothers published his entire series of stories in a book entitled *Uncle Tom's Children.* Its artistic genius and its penetrating awareness of the painful truths of racism and poverty in America were undeniable. The book achieved immediate and nearly universal acclaim, and Wright soon received a Guggenheim Fellowship, a cash prize to help finance the writing of his next work.

In fact, by the time he had been awarded the fellowship, Wright had nearly completed that book, an ambitious novel that combined elements of subtle psychological analysis with powerful Marxian social criticism. Wright published this work in 1940; it is called *Native Son.* It is Wright's greatest book, and also one of the most important American novels of the Twentieth Century. As Wright himself explains in "How 'Bigger' Was Born"—a brilliant essay that is now published with the novel—he wanted *Native Son* to shock his white liberal admirers. He set his stark tale in the frozen Chicago ghetto, and is thereby able to reveal just how deeply divided *all* of America was, not only in the backward, faraway South—the setting of the stories in *Uncle Tom's Children*—but in the great modern cities of the North as well.

Wright's uncompromising book made him a famous writer, and readers were hungry to hear his own story. He responded with another masterwork, *Black Boy,* the first part of his autobiography, in which he included a powerful essay about segregation, "The Ethics of Living Jim Crow." (The second part of the autobiography, titled *American Hunger,* was not fully published until after Wright's death.) *Black Boy* appeared in 1945, and was even more successful than *Native Son.* Richard Wright was now looked upon as a spokesman for an entire generation of African Americans.

With his words and with his actions, Richard Wright continued to struggle throughout his life against injustice. However, he left the Communist Party during the Second World War. He was repelled not by the idea of socialism, but by the narrow dogmatism of Joseph Stalin, the leader of the Soviet Union, and his adherents who controlled the Party in America. Within a few years of Wright's break from the Communist Party, the Cold War against the Soviet Union began. The domestic implications of this cold war affected Wright directly, because Congress began investigating American Communists in a campaign of intimidation that would come to be known as "McCarthyism," after Senator Joseph McCarthy, one of the most ruthless anti-communists. Wright himself had for a long time been under F.B.I. surveillance, and even though he was no longer a Communist, he was still regarded by the government as a potentially dangerous subversive. He knew that he would soon be called to testify before the "House Un-American Activities Committee," a Congressional body, where he would be asked to denounce his former Communist friends. He also knew that if he refused, he could be jailed.

The very real threat of government repression, combined with his increasing weariness of racism in American society, led Richard Wright to seek exile in France. In 1947, he moved to Paris, and he would spend almost all of the rest of his life in Europe. He associated there with French philosophers Albert Camus and Jean-Paul Sartre, and tried for a time to build with them a new revolutionary movement. He was also interested in their existentialist philosophy, and he explored themes of freedom and alienation in *The Outsider*, a novel published in 1953.

Toward the end of his life, Wright became involved, along with his friends George Padmore and Frantz Fanon, in the struggles of African countries to be rid of colonial rule. These men injected new life into Pan-Africanism, a movement which sought a revolutionary third path for African peoples, independent of capitalism and communism.

Richard Wright died suddenly in Paris on November 28, 1960, at the age of fifty-two. He left behind an enduring literary legacy which yet challenges readers to delve deeply into questions of racism, poverty, and human freedom. His ashes now rest in Père Lachaise cemetery, in Paris, far from his race-divided native shore. Yet that place is appropriate. Near his remains lie the graves of

Victor Hugo and Honoré de Balzac, France's greatest authors. Richard Wright may have been of a different age than those nineteenth century giants, but he was of the same race, the human race, and his vision of humanity was equally as vast.

Historical Background

The novel takes place in the city of Chicago in the late 1930s, during the Great Depression. It is a time when many thousands of nearly destitute African-American families are migrating from the South, in search of employment in the cities of the North. Many find their way to Chicago, where they are crowded into the city's South Side ghetto, strictly segregated from the white parts of town. The Depression is a stormy period in American history, as millions of African Americans and poor white workers struggle to survive. The American Communist Party is at the height of its power, and is attempting to break down racial barriers and win prosperity for blacks and whites through overthrow of the rule of the wealthy classes. The NAACP (National Association for the Advancement of Colored People) is also organizing at this time, but favors more moderate methods.

While *Native Son* deals centrally with American racism in general, one important aspect of racism that the author confronts directly is related to sex. For centuries, American racists have believed that white women are in danger of being raped by black men. Many black men have been lynched (murdered), after being falsely accused of rape by frenzied mobs of whites. In one famous case in the 1930s, nine innocent teenaged boys were convicted of raping a white girl in Alabama, and all were condemned to die. Known as the "Scottsboro Boys," they were saved from execution after years of mass protest. However, only four were set free. The remaining five served prison terms of varying lengths. Richard Wright himself participated in the movement to free them, and the Communist Party handled their legal defense.

Native Son was a Book-of-the-Month Club selection, and sold over 200,000 copies in its first three weeks. Most critics recognized the importance of the work right away, although many readers were indeed shocked by the intense violence of the story. Ralph Ellison, who would later write the acclaimed novel *Invisible Man,* remarked,

"In Wright's *Native Son* we have the first philosophical novel by an American Negro. This work possesses an artistry, penetration of thought, and sheer emotional power that places it into the front rank of American fiction" (*New Masses*, August 5, 1941). In 1941 the NAACP awarded the author of *Native Son* its prestigious Spingarn Medal.

Master List of Characters

Bigger Thomas—*The main character is a 20-year-old African American who lives with his family in a single tenement room on Chicago's strictly segregated South Side.*

Mrs. Thomas—*Bigger's mother, who brought her family north about eight years earlier, sometime after white men killed Bigger's father in Mississippi.*

Buddy Thomas—*Bigger's younger brother, and the youngest of the three Thomas children; he is fiercely loyal to Bigger.*

Vera Thomas—*Bigger's younger sister.*

Gus, G.H., and Jack Harding—*Bigger's friends, who hang around a South Side poolroom.*

Doc—*Owner of the poolroom.*

Bessie Mears—*Bigger's girlfriend; She is a servant and housekeeper for rich white families.*

Reverend Hammond—*The pastor of Mrs. Thomas' church.*

Henry G. Dalton—*Chicago real estate millionaire who hires Bigger as his chauffeur; He has given five million dollars to African-American education, yet makes a fortune renting rat-infested rooms to black families at inflated prices.*

Mrs. Dalton—*Wife of Henry Dalton; 51-years-old, blind and frail; She holds what she believes are liberal views towards African Americans.*

Mary Dalton—*Twenty-three-years-old; She is Mr. and Mrs. Dalton's only child. Despite her wealth and her disapproving parents, she sympathizes strongly with the Communist Party and its attitude toward African Americans.*

Peggy O'Flagherty—*The Daltons' Irish cook and housekeeper.*

Mr. Britten—*A private investigator whom Mr. Dalton hires to investigate Mary Dalton's disappearance.*

Mrs. Patterson—*Mrs. Dalton's maid.*

Mrs. Rawlson—*Mrs. Dalton's aged mother.*

Jan Erlone—*Mary Dalton's boyfriend; a member of the Communist Party, and the executive secretary of Labor Defenders, the Communist Party's legal arm.*

Boris A. Max—*The Jewish lawyer from Labor Defenders, a Communist group, who agrees to defend Bigger.*

David A. Buckley—*Illinois state's attorney who is up for re-election, and who prosecutes Bigger.*

Stenographer—*Buckley uses him to record Bigger's jailhouse confession.*

Deputy Coroner—*He conducts the preliminary inquest of Bigger's case.*

Chief Justice Alvin C. Hanley—*The judge who decides Bigger's case.*

H. M. O'Dorsey—*Governor of Illinois.*

Mayor Ditz—*Mayor of Chicago.*

Glenman—*Chief of police.*

Horace Minton—*Superintendent of the school system.*

Calvin H. Robinson—*The police psychiatrist.*

Mr. Britten's assistants—*three otherwise unidentified assistants.*

White vigilantes—*Deputized by Chief Glenman to hunt for Bigger.*

Many unnamed newspaper reporters—*Cover the story of Bigger's trial.*

Summary of the Novel

Native Son takes place in Chicago. All the action is confined to a few weeks in the winter of an unspecified year in the late 1930s. Twenty-year-old Bigger Thomas is living in a tenement room in the South Side ghetto with his mother and younger sister and brother.

Book One: Fear

As the novel begins, Bigger's mother urges him to accept a job that is being offered by Henry Dalton, a wealthy white man who owns much of the property in the ghetto. She tells Bigger that if he refuses, the family will be denied relief (welfare), and be unable to pay rent or buy food. Bigger agrees to see Mr. Dalton, but first visits his friends at a poolroom, where they plan out their latest and most daring robbery. Although the plan to rob a white-owned delicatessen is Bigger's own, he becomes frightened and ruins the plan.

Bigger goes to see Mr. Dalton at his mansion, and accepts the job of chauffeur. He is to be paid $25 per week, which is a good salary for those times. He is also given a room to live in. Nevertheless, he is extremely nervous, because he will now have to live his life amongst white people, whom he knows from experience are racists. He has even brought his gun to the interview. Bigger's nervousness turns to near panic when Mary Dalton, Mr. Dalton's beautiful, 23-year-old daughter, appears. Mary has begun to question her father's wealth, and she is sympathetic to communism. She tries to speak to Bigger as an equal, rather than as a servant, but Bigger is worried that such talk might cause him to lose his job.

Bigger's first task on his new job turns into an unparalleled nightmare. He drives Mary to see Jan Erlone, her communist boyfriend. The three then drive to the South Side, and eat in one of Bigger's favorite restaurants. Jan and Mary ask Bigger to eat with them, and Bigger does so reluctantly. Jan buys a bottle of rum, and when the three leave the restaurant, they all drink from it. Bigger drops Jan off near his home, and then drives Mary home. Mary is quite intoxicated at this point, and Bigger helps her to her room, ever fearful that he might be caught with a drunken white girl in his arms. Suddenly, Mary's blind mother appears at the door of the bedroom, just as Bigger is putting Mary to bed. Wild with fear, Bigger puts a pillow over Mary's head to stifle her moans, so that Mrs. Dalton will come no closer and discover him. When Mrs. Dalton leaves, Bigger takes the pillow away, and Mary is dead. Bigger brings her body to the basement, and shoves her into the furnace. He has to hack off her head to make the body fit.

Book Two: Flight

In this section of the novel, Bigger first tries to deceive the Daltons about their missing daughter by implicating Jan in her disappearance. He enlists his girlfriend Bessie in a plan to extort ransom money from the family, and sends a note to Mr. Dalton asking for $10,000, which he signs "Red," to make everyone think the communists have Mary. Newspaper reporters are allowed into the Dalton's basement, and one of them discovers unburned pieces of human bone, and Mary's earring. Bigger witnesses the discovery and flees. He goes to Bessie's house to call off the ransom plan, and the two hide out in an abandoned building. There Bigger rapes Bessie, and then murders her, so that she cannot be interrogated by the authorities. Five thousand police officers conduct a brutal house-to-house search of the ghetto, and Bigger is soon caught.

Book Three: Fate

As the Chicago newspapers fill their pages with horrifying racist imagery, much of the city's white population is whipped into a frenzy of hate, and the call for Bigger's death grows louder and louder. Jan, who has forgiven Bigger for murdering his girlfriend and then trying to implicate him in the crime, helps Bigger get a lawyer. He is Boris Max, a Jewish Communist. In the course of preparing Bigger's case, lawyer and client actually become close, and their relationship enables Bigger to begin to understand his own actions. At the end of Bigger's trial, Max makes an electrifying appeal for his life—much of which was cut out of the first edition of the novel. The appeal fails, and Bigger is condemned to die. In their last meeting, Bigger tells Max that his crimes must have had a good purpose, or else he would not have risked his life committing them. Max is clearly shaken by Bigger's reasoning, and the two men part, still in separate worlds.

Estimated Reading Time

The average silent reading rate for a secondary student is 250 to 300 words per minute. Since each page of the 1993 HarperPerennial edition has up to 350 words, an average student might take two minutes to read one page. At that rate, the total reading time for the 500-page novel is between 16 and 17 hours.

There are no chapters, but the author has broken his novel into three "books": "Fear" (108 pages), "Flight" (206 pages), and "Fate" (188 pages). Try reading the first book in two or three sittings, and the second and third in four or five sittings each.

Native Son

Book 1: Fear

New Characters:

Bigger Thomas: *the protagonist; a poor, 20-year-old African American*

Mrs. Thomas: *Bigger's mother*

Buddy Thomas: *Bigger's younger brother*

Vera Thomas: *Bigger's younger sister*

Gus, G.H., and Jack Harding: *Bigger's poolroom friends*

Doc: *owner of the poolroom*

Bessie Mears: *Bigger's girlfriend*

Henry G. Dalton: *white Chicago millionaire and Bigger's employer*

Mrs. Dalton: *Henry Dalton's blind wife*

Mary Dalton: *Henry Dalton's 23-year-old daughter*

Peggy O'Flagherty: *the Daltons' Irish cook and housekeeper*

Mrs. Patterson: *Mrs. Dalton's maid*

Jan Erlone: *Mary Dalton's Communist boyfriend*

David A. Buckley: *Illinois state's attorney, who is up for reelection*

Summary

It is winter in Chicago during the Depression in the late 1930s. The Thomas family awakens in their one room tenement apartment in the South Side ghetto. At once, Bigger Thomas' mother and sister spy a large rat scurrying around the floor. Responding to their fearful cries, Bigger repeatedly tries to kill the rat with an iron skillet, finally succeeding on the third try. Bigger then taunts his sister Vera with the bloody carcass, causing her to faint. Bigger's mother scolds her son for his cruelty and insensitivity, and reveals that the family is on relief (welfare). The relief agency has offered Bigger a job, and has threatened to cut off the family's food benefit if Bigger does not accept it. Reluctantly, Bigger agrees to see Mr. Dalton, his prospective employer, about the job.

Bigger then proceeds to his hangout, a nearby poolroom, to meet his friends, Gus, G.H., and Jack. For months Bigger and his friends have been planning to rob Blum's, a local delicatessen, but all are scared to do it because the owner is white. Rather than admit his own fears, Bigger taunts Gus, accusing him of cowardice, secretly hoping that he will back out, and so ruin the plan. Gus does not back out, however, and a tense agreement is reached to meet back at the poolroom at 3 p.m.

Bigger and Jack leave the poolroom and go to a movie theater, where they masturbate in the darkness, before the show begins. The first picture is a newsreel about "debutantes", rich, unmarried young society girls, vacationing in Florida. Mary Dalton, Mr. Dalton's daughter, is featured in the film, and as Bigger and Jack ogle her cavorting on the beach in a bathing suit, they learn that she has recently scandalized her parents by taking a communist for a boyfriend. After viewing *Trader Horn*, a sensational film about Africa, Bigger and Jack part to fetch their guns for the planned robbery, and then both meet G.H. at the poolroom. While Gus is not late, he arrives last, and Bigger pounces on him at once. Again, Bigger projects his own fears of robbing a white man onto Gus, and viciously attacks his friend, knife in hand. Gus manages to flee, and the plan is ruined. G.H. tells Bigger, "I reckon that is what you wanted." Doc, the poolroom owner, throws Bigger out.

Later, Bigger proceeds to his job interview, taking a streetcar to the rich, white neighborhood where the Daltons live. He takes

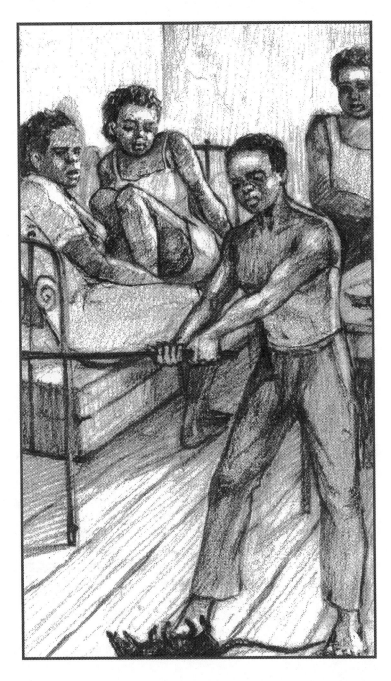

his gun along, deciding it will make him feel safe. He is greeted by the Daltons' cook and housekeeper, Peggy O'Flagherty, and soon encounters Mr. Dalton and his frail, blind wife. Bigger is nervous and fidgety as Mr. Dalton questions him about his past. It is revealed that Bigger has been in reform school for stealing tires, but Mr. Dalton offers him the job of family chauffeur anyway, at the ample salary of $25 per week, plus room and board.

Bigger accepts the job, and just then Mary Dalton appears, and immediately starts talking about how Bigger should be in a union. Her naive political remarks make Bigger fearful that he will lose his job. After Mary leaves, Mr. Dalton informs Bigger that he is a supporter of the NAACP (National Association for the Advancement of Colored People), a moderate organization dedicated to improving the status of African Americans. Bigger later learns from Peggy O'Flagherty that Mr. Dalton has given five million dollars to Negro education, an act that is apparently at odds with Bigger's suspicion that he is also Chicago's principal ghetto slumlord. Peggy feeds Bigger a delicious meal, and shows him how to take care of the mansion's large basement furnace, which will be another of his duties. Bigger then goes to his new, comfortable room, and relaxes, content before his first assignment.

Bigger is to drive Mary Dalton to a University lecture that night, and on the way to the garage, he encounters Mrs. Dalton, who expresses the hope that Bigger himself will one day return to school. Bigger is painfully self-conscious during every encounter he has with white people, but he is most troubled by Mary Dalton, whose behavior he finds unpredictable and unsettling. Once in the car, she tells Bigger that she is not going to the University. Instead, she has him take her to meet Jan Erlone, her Communist boyfriend. Jan is even more intent than Mary is on treating Bigger as an equal, and immediately he breaks many of the taboos of racism. He shakes Bigger's hand, and asks Bigger to call him by his first name. He also tells Bigger that he (Jan) will drive to their next destination, and he and Mary squeeze into the front seat of the car, with Bigger between them.

Jan and Mary want to eat in the ghetto, and Bigger directs them to Ernie's Kitchen Shack, a restaurant he knows on the South Side. When they arrive, Jan and Mary implore Bigger to eat with them,

and Bigger does so with extreme reluctance. Inside, Bigger's girl-friend, Bessie Mears, greets him, but he is uncomfortable in this situation and virtually ignores her. Jan questions Bigger about his childhood, and Bigger reveals that he is from the South, and hints that his father was murdered there by a white mob. Jan then discusses communism with Bigger, and mentions the Scottsboro case. As they eat the food they have ordered, the three drink beer at first, and then rum. Mary mentions to Bigger that she is going to Detroit the next day, and that he must take down her trunk and drive her to the train station in the morning.

They all continue to drink from the bottle of rum after they leave the restaurant. Bigger drives as Jan and Mary discuss politics in the back seat. Mary happily agrees to supply bail money for several Communists who have been arrested, and then reveals to Jan that she intends to join the Communist Party in the near future. She wants to work among Negroes, she says, because they are the most oppressed sector of the population. At this point Bigger is feeling warm from the rum, but Jan is drunk and Mary is even more intoxicated. The couple kiss and caress in the back seat, and Bigger struggles not to become sexually aroused. Soon, Jan notes that it is 1 a.m., and that he'd better go. Bigger drops him near his home, and all three take one last long pull from the rum bottle. Jan gives Bigger some communist literature to read and says goodbye.

Mary, extremely intoxicated at this time, sprawls out in the front seat, and leans her head on Bigger's shoulder. When they arrive at the Dalton home, Mary is unconscious, and Bigger must rouse her and help her to her room. He takes her in his arms and begins to move her into the house. His terror at being seen touching a white woman is somewhat mitigated by the effects of the alcohol, and his mood swings between a sobering fear and sexual arousal. When they do arrive in her darkened room, Bigger begins to kiss Mary, and Mary responds, grinding her hips against him. Bigger caresses her breasts, but just as he lays her down on the bed, blind Mrs. Dalton appears at the doorway. Bigger at once becomes wild with fear. Mary's semi-conscious mumbles are attracting Mrs. Dalton and beckoning her closer, to where she might discover Bigger, so he puts a pillow over Mary's head to stifle her. Mary struggles, so Bigger pushes down harder. Mrs. Dalton continues to

approach, until she smells liquor in the air, at which point she re-
coils, exclaiming, "You're dead drunk! You *stink* with whiskey!"
Bigger begins to relax after Mrs. Dalton leaves the room, but he
soon discovers that he has suffocated Mary to death.

Though he is terrified, his survival instinct is strong, and he
begins to assemble a plan of action to avoid being caught. He knows
that murdering a white girl, whatever the circumstances, means
certain death. He begins to think of a way to implicate Jan and the
Communists in the crime. He also puts the body in the trunk, which
Mary has half-packed for her trip to Detroit, and carries it downstairs to the basement. Once there, he decides to burn the body in
the furnace. He stuffs Mary inside, but her head will not fit. He hacks
it off with a knife and hatchet, and tosses it in the flames. He plans
to tell anyone who asks that Jan accompanied him and Mary home,
and that he left them kissing in the car, which is still in the driveway.
When he checks the car, he finds Mary's purse, and inside it, a thick
roll of bills. He keeps the purse, and then goes home to his mother's
house, planning to take the trunk to the station in the morning.

Analysis

Native Son is regarded today as one of the greatest American
novels of the twentieth century. When it first appeared, many critics compared the book to John Steinbeck's *The Grapes of Wrath*,
which had been published a year earlier, and which powerfully
described the miserable plight of thousands of drought-stricken
Oklahoma farmers who were then migrating to California in search
of work. In fact both novels are examples of *naturalism*, a literary
style that first emerged in France in the late nineteenth century,
and was adopted by many American writers in the first half of the
twentieth century. Naturalist authors usually focused their writing
on the harsher aspects of human existence, on issues such as poverty and the struggles of poor working people. They attempted to
examine in their work the conditions of human suffering and to
analyze its causes. They also professed to be describing the world
around them just as it appears, even photographically, without
romantic embellishment.

When Richard Wright moved to Chicago, he encountered there
the works of all the important American naturalist authors, such

as Stephen Crane, Sinclair Lewis, James Farrell, and Frank Norris. He had a special affection, however, for Theodore Dreiser, the most renowned American exponent of naturalism, and *Native Son* adopts much of the literary methodology found in *An American Tragedy*, Dreiser's most ambitious novel.

Another important influence on *Native Son* was the work of the Russian novelist Fyodor Dostoevsky. Wright was particularly impressed by Dostoevsky's *Crime and Punishment*, a book which explores the inner, psychological life of its characters, and the choices they face in the outside world, as well as the notion of individual "free will." These are themes that were later taken up by French philosophers Jean-Paul Sartre and Albert Camus, existentialists whose friendship Wright sought out later in his life.

The explosive impact which *Native Son* had on American society in 1940 was therefore partly created by Richard Wright's masterful blending of two literary methods—his unrelentingly realistic, or *naturalist* portrayal of the external conditions of ghetto life, and his revealing disclosure of the psychology, the *inner* life, of his main character, Bigger Thomas. Without a doubt, Bigger Thomas is Richard Wright's most important literary creation, and the reason *Native Son* has a lasting place in our literature.

In "How Bigger Was Born," Wright's penetrating essay that is now published with the novel, he describes two sources that led him to create Bigger. First was his memory of several tough young black men whom he had encountered as a boy in the South. These youths bullied other African Americans, but more importantly, they openly defied the strict laws of segregation separating blacks from whites, and often met with violent ends for doing so. The second force which inspired him to create Bigger Thomas was the white public's reaction to his earlier book, *Uncle Tom's Children*. It is a collection of stories about the terror of segregation which African Americans face in the South. It was so well received by liberal whites that Wright realized he had created a book "which even bankers' daughters could read and weep over and feel good about." "I swore to myself," Wright continued, "that if ever I wrote another book, no one would weep over it; that it would be so hard and deep that they would have to face it without the consolation of tears." In the North, where there was no legal segregation, African Americans

were still forced to live apart from white society. They were being crowded into ghettos, made to accept the lowest-paying jobs (if they could find work at all), and were subjected to police persecution for the slightest protest against their oppressive existence. Wright wants us to see that Bigger's entire experience of life, in the North as well as in the South, has been violent and fear-filled, and that this crushingly brutal experience created a violent and fear-filled character. Wright believed that white liberals, who might donate money to Negro causes, or condemn Southern segregation—while themselves enjoying the privileges of white society in the North—have no idea just how deep lie the causes of racial oppression, or just how shattering that oppression is for the vast ghettoized population.

From the moment Bigger Thomas first appears in the novel, the reader is made aware of his hard and dehumanizing existence. A rat is loose in the Thomas family's squalid tenement room, and Bigger, barely awake, must kill it with a frying pan. It is a scene bereft of human dignity, and a fitting first look at a character who has little if any chance of ever achieving it.

Wright draws for the reader a vivid and grim picture of Bigger's world—the Depression-era Chicago ghetto. It is a world whose inhabitants are entirely at the mercy of forces beyond their control. The realty company actually charges African Americans more in rent than they would pay for comparable quarters in a poor white neighborhood, but they may not move outside the ghetto. Food costs more in grocery stores in the ghetto. African-American men are often out of work entirely, and their wives and daughters must work as servants in the homes of rich whites. The anxieties of living on the edge of utter destitution create in many ghetto-dwellers a fearful, timid attitude. Like Mrs. Thomas, they work hard and do everything in their power to hold the line against ruin. Bigger, however, has developed a different attitude. Despite his meager education, a complex psychology has grown inside him, and the reader is made aware of this psychology partly through his often disturbing actions, but more by the thoughts the author has made him express.

Bigger is angry, rebellious, and brutish. He bullies his family and his friends. He has a gun, and has committed robberies of

black-owned stores. He plots with his friends to rob a white-owned store, but here his rebelliousness hits up against its own source and limitation. When blacks are victimized by crimes, the all-white police force does little to pursue the criminals. However when a white store is robbed, particularly if it is robbed by blacks, then the police will do everything in their power to catch and imprison the culprits. A life of crime is therefore a dead end for Bigger, and he realizes he must take the job at the Daltons' house or starve. He is conscious of his dilemma, and "maddened" by the thought that he does not have a "wider choice of action."

When he wrote *Native Son*, Richard Wright was not a black nationalist, but a communist. He did not believe that all whites were evil, but that the system of capitalism oppressed blacks and poor whites alike, and also set one against the other by encouraging racism, so the two oppressed groups would not unite. However, Wright wants us to know that America has created many Biggers, who only see before them one undifferentiated, hateful, and all-powerful white race. Bigger tells his friend Gus, "You know where the white folks live?…Right down here in my stomach." He is ever-conscious of the source of his fear, and when he lashes out at fellow African Americans, he does so really because he is ashamed of their pitiable and degraded condition.

Bigger's terrible encounter with Jan and Mary is of course the climax of this section of the novel. The rich girl and her Communist boyfriend do try to reach out to Bigger, but their attempt at friendship is totally inadequate when set in the larger context of the unforgiving race-divided reality in which Bigger must live. Even an ordinary gesture, like Jan's attempt to shake Bigger's hand, violates a racial taboo, and therefore Bigger is only made angrier and more uncomfortable when he is in their presence. He thinks that they are either crazy or are trying to mock him, and make him feel just how much the color of his skin sets him apart. When he does let down his guard a little, and drinks rum with Jan and Mary, it only sets off an awful chain of circumstances at the end of which Bigger inadvertently suffocates Mary. "Inadvertently" is an important word here, because the act that will define the rest of Bigger's life—the killing of Mary Dalton—is not really a conscious action at all. He does not mean to kill Mary, but only to quiet her moans, so

that Mrs. Dalton will not detect his presence in her room. In an ideal sense, just before the shocking crime, Mary and Bigger are simply two intoxicated young people who express their mutual physical desire by beginning to kiss and caress. However in the ugly race-divided real world, Bigger is crossing the most forbidding and terrifying line of all. If he was caught even kissing a drunken Mary Dalton, he could be accused of rape and sent to the electric chair. Some might argue that the Daltons would not have condemned Bigger in this way, but Bigger has no way of knowing how they might act, he only knows that other African-American men have been killed for less.

Study Questions

1. Where and during what time in American history does the novel take place?

2. Who are the Thomases, and where and how do they live?

3. Who are the Daltons, and where and how do they live?

4. What job does Mr. Dalton offer Bigger?

5. What is one of the sources of Mr. Dalton's wealth?

6. What views toward African Americans does Mr. Dalton profess to hold?

7. Why does Mary Dalton make Bigger so uncomfortable?

8. Who is Jan Erlone, and what is his political affiliation and philosophy?

9. Why do Jan and Mary try so hard to befriend Bigger, and why is Bigger reluctant to accept their friendship?

10. Why does Bigger plan to implicate Jan in Mary's death?

Answers

1. The novel is set in Chicago, in the late 1930s, during the Great Depression. It is a time of great poverty in America, and much social unrest.

2. The Thomases are an African-American family. Mrs. Thomas lives with her sons Bigger and Buddy, and her daughter Vera,

in a one-room tenement apartment in Chicago's South Side ghetto. The family is very poor, and is on relief (welfare).

3.   The Daltons are a rich white family; Henry and Mrs. Dalton live in a mansion in the wealthy part of town, with Mary, their only child, and several servants.

4.   Bigger is offered and accepts the job of Dalton family chauffeur. He is also to tend the mansion's furnace.

5.   Bigger has heard that Mr. Dalton is the owner of the South Side Real Estate Company, to which the Thomases and many other African-American families in the ghetto must pay rent.

6.   Mr. Dalton is professedly liberal toward African Americans. He is a supporter of the National Association for the Advancement of Colored People, and has donated five million dollars to Negro education.

7.   In her own naive way, Mary tries to treat Bigger as an equal. Bigger fears that her overtures to him might cause him to lose his job, because such behavior challenges the strict rules of racist society, which he must obey in order to live. Her actions are especially threatening because she is a white girl, and Bigger knows that African-American men are often killed for associating with white women.

8.   Jan Erlone is Mary's boyfriend. He is a young white member of the Chicago branch of the American Communist Party. As a Communist, Jan believes that the system of private ownership known as capitalism is responsible for both poverty and racism. Communists believe that to rid society of these ills, capitalism itself must be overthrown and replaced by a system of public ownership, known as socialism.

9.   Jan and Mary, each in their own way, seek to break down the barriers between the races. Although Bigger has never met white people who behave as they do, he remains suspicious because he knows that whites can be very dangerous—his father, after all, was murdered in the South by white men.

10. Bigger knows from reading the newspapers that many white people hate Communists, and since Jan is a Communist,

their suspicions might be easily directed against Jan, and away from Bigger himself.

Suggested Essay Topics

1. Compare and contrast Bigger's attitude toward the world around him with Mrs. Thomas'.

2. Bigger and his friends discuss the choices in life available to whites, as opposed to those available to African Americans. They also "play white," a game they have invented. In light of the interaction that takes place on these pages, what does "freedom of choice" mean to Bigger, and how important is it to him?

3. Mr. Dalton and Jan Erlone both profess to be friendly toward African Americans, yet they are hostile to each other. Compare and contrast their attitudes toward African Americans and explain their mutual hostility.

4. Discuss Bigger's reasoning for stifling Mary's moans, rather than simply admitting to Mrs. Dalton that he had to help her daughter upstairs because she was drunk.

Book 2: Flight

New Characters:

Mr. Britten: *a private investigator hired by Mr. Dalton to find Mary*

Britten's assistants: *three otherwise unidentified white men*

Various newspapermen: *present in the Dalton home, reporting on Mary's disappearance*

Mayor Ditz: *mayor of Chicago*

Glenman: *chief of police*

Horace Minton: *superintendent of schools*

White vigilantes: *deputized by Glenman to hunt for Bigger*

Summary

Early the next morning, Bigger awakes in his house, horrified at what he has done. Fear and the desire to flee are always with him now, but he nevertheless continues to act according to his original plan. He disposes of Mary's purse and a bloody knife in a nearby garbage pail. He keeps her money. He returns to his house for his clothes, and his mother wakes up. She is happy that he has such a good job, but she does not understand why he remains so sullen, or why he insists he came home at 2 a.m., when she knows he came home at 4 a.m.. Bigger eats with his family. Buddy, his brother, suspects something is wrong, especially when he retrieves a wad of bills Bigger has dropped on the floor. Bigger warns Buddy to keep quiet about the money, and takes his suitcase and heads out to the Daltons' house. First, he stops briefly at the corner drugstore, where he encounters Gus, G.H., and Jack. He rekindles his friendships, and with Mary's money buys them beer and cigarettes, and gives each a dollar bill.

At the Dalton house, he finds only Peggy is awake. It is Sunday morning, and Mr. and Mrs. Dalton are sleeping late. Peggy wants to know why the car is in the driveway, and Bigger tells her that Mary told him to leave it there, and that Jan was with her at the time. He checks the furnace and is satisfied that Mary's body has burned up in the night. When Peggy discovers that Mary is not at home, she is puzzled, because she knows Mary must leave on a train for Detroit soon. She tells Bigger to take her trunk to the railroad station anyway, which he does. Mrs. Dalton comes downstairs, worried about Mary. She interviews Peggy and then speaks to Bigger, who has returned from the station. Her concern about Mary heightens when Bigger tells her that Jan was present at the house last night. She does not at all suspect Bigger, and gives him the rest of the day off.

Bigger goes to see Bessie, who is initially jealous of Mary, but Bigger assures her that the white people he was with at Ernie's Kitchen Shack the previous night are only his employers. Bessie softens, and the two make tender love. However, Bessie is suspicious of the money Bigger shows her, and remarks eerily that the Daltons happen to live in the same neighborhood as Richard Loeb. Loeb, along with his partner in crime Leopold, were two rich youths

who committed a spectacular murder in 1924, and then tried to extract ransom money from the victim's father. Bigger eventually tells Bessie that Mary has eloped with her Communist boyfriend and that her parents have no idea where she is. He also suggests that he and Bessie could extort ransom too, the way Leopold and Loeb attempted to do. Bessie's fears about what Bigger has done to Mary mount, and she begins to cry. She is certain that she will be drawn into Bigger's criminal scheme even though she wants no part of it. Bigger assures her that everything will be all right, and then he returns to the Dalton house.

Mr. Dalton probes Bigger further, but Mrs. Dalton signals him to stop, out of embarrassment that their Negro servant has seen Mary drunk. The Daltons then instruct Bigger to return to the railroad station and retrieve Mary's trunk, which has of course remained there unclaimed. On the drive over he works out his plan to extort $10,000 ransom from the Daltons. When Bigger returns with the trunk, he is again interrogated, this time by Mr. Britten, a private investigator Mr. Dalton has hired. While playing the role of a simple-minded servant, Bigger cleverly manipulates Britten's hatred of Communists, and gets him to think that Jan Erlone is responsible for Mary's disappearance. When Britten belligerently insists that Bigger is a Communist, Mr. Dalton comes to Bigger's aid, assuring Britten that it is not true.

Bigger goes to his room and has a nightmare about his predicament. He is awakened by Britten and Mr. Dalton, who bring Jan into his room. Jan is shocked that Bigger has lied, and he tells Britten and Mr. Dalton the truth, but they do not believe him. Mr. Dalton offers him money for the safe return of Mary, but Jan is outraged and storms out. When Britten and Mr. Dalton leave, Bigger decides to go see Bessie and initiate his ransom plan. Outside he is at once accosted by Jan, who demands to know why he is lying, and where Mary is. Bigger draws his gun and chases him off. At Bessie's, Bigger carefully composes a ransom note, and signs it "Red," adding the hammer-and-sickle emblem of the Communist Party to the signature. Bessie now knows that Bigger has killed Mary. She is terrified, but is resigned to helping Bigger in his scheme, which she assumes will land her in jail. Bigger finds an abandoned ghetto building to serve as the lookout point for the ransom drop,

and Bessie reluctantly agrees to go there on the following night to retrieve the money.

Bigger returns to the Dalton house and slips the kidnap note under the front door. Britten, now in the company of his assistants, again interrogates Bigger. Suddenly, a crowd of newspapermen bursts into the Dalton basement, revealing that Jan has been arrested and word of Mary's disappearance is already in the papers. They also reveal that Jan is now publicly accusing Bigger of lying. Mr. Dalton then appears, and announces to the press that he has ordered Jan's release, that his daughter has been kidnapped, and that he intends to pay off the kidnappers just as he has been instructed to do in the ransom note. After Mr. Dalton leaves, the reporters discover that Jan has refused to leave jail while he is still under a cloud of suspicion, and insists that he has a dozen witnesses to verify his story. Bigger continues to fool Britten as well as the reporters, answering all questions reluctantly, in the guise of a scared and ignorant servant. Peggy comes downstairs and tells Bigger to clean out the furnace, because there is not enough heat upstairs. Terrified that Mary's remains are buried in those ashes, Bigger instead dumps more coal on the fire, choking it and filling the basement with smoke. As the reporters gag on soot-filled air, one of them seizes a shovel from the panicked Bigger and begins to empty the furnace's ash-bin. The reporter finds unburned human bones and an earring in the ashes, and calls out for the others to see. Bigger at once realizes his position; he gets his gun and flees the Dalton house.

He at once goes to Bessie's to call off the ransom plan, and tells her that his crimes have been discovered. Bessie is terrified now, and certain that she is about to be arrested. Bigger uses her fear to keep her with him, and the two flee to a freezing cold, abandoned building. There Bessie comes to realize at last that she is innocent, and that Bigger has been the cause of her troubles. Bigger, however, has decided that she is a liability, now that the police are after him. He rapes her, and then murders her brutally. He throws her body down the airshaft of the building.

Bigger realizes he has only seven cents. He forgot to take Mary's money out of the pocket of Bessie's dress before throwing her down the airshaft. He goes out and steals a newspaper, and reads the

lurid, racist stories about his crime. Five thousand police officers have surrounded the ghetto and are conducting a house-to-house search. Blacks have been beaten by mobs. The police are organizing vigilante squads to help in the search. Most disturbing to Bigger are the reports which indicate that the authorities think Bigger raped Mary, and then murdered her and burned her body to disguise the crime. He now knows they will kill him if they capture him, and he can see from a map of the search printed in the paper that it will not be long before he is caught.

Bigger moves to an unrented flat in an occupied building, where he will be safer, and also warmer. He gets another paper and sees the pictures of himself, and more lurid stories of how the entire black population of the city is under siege by thousands of frenzied white manhunters. Suddenly, he hears a resident in the next apartment exclaim, "They's comin!" As the vigilantes approach, there is only one way for Bigger to go: up to the snowy roof. He hides there, but the vigilantes soon find the roof as well. Bigger still has his pistol with him, and he uses it to knock the first vigilante unconscious. More follow, however, and Bigger is soon spotted. One vigilante shoots at him, and others track him with searchlights as he clambers over connected rooftops. Finally, when Bigger is cornered, he climbs to the top of a great water tower, where he is shot at with bullets and canisters of tear-gas. He is numb with cold, but manages to return fire. He keeps track of how many bullets he has, because he wants to be sure to have one left to use on himself. However, his hunters turn a hose on him, and he loses the gun, and then falls from the icy ledge of the water tower to the roof below. Amid the murderous cries of his captors, Bigger is dragged down into the street with great brutality.

Analysis

In this section of the novel, the author reveals Bigger's psychology in great detail. Much of what Bigger comes to believe about himself, his crime, and the white world, has truth in it, but the author also allows the willing reader to see things Bigger does not see. Wright has created a world where the points of view of each of the characters are limited and all suffer at one time or another from "blindness." In the first section of the novel, Bigger looks at his

younger sister, innocent but born poor and helpless, and feels she is "blind." He realizes that he himself has been blind, when, after having seen how the Daltons live, he "sees" his own rat-infested tenement home as for the first time. Bigger also sees that Bessie, too, who works hard all day and yearns only for the physical release of alcohol and parties, is trapped and therefore blind. Mrs. Dalton, Mary Dalton's kindly mother, is *literally* blind. She can function unaided only in the Dalton mansion, a private world of great wealth which insulates the Dalton family, and prevents them from "seeing" the poverty outside, on which that wealth rests.

With all the references to blindness and sight, whether of the symbolic or literal varieties, the author is illuminating for the reader the relationship of the perceptions of the characters (the subjects) with the actual world (the object) they are perceiving. The actual world is in fact more than an object, it is one, and includes in it all the perceivers as well as all they are perceiving. Each character's perception, however, is limited, and therefore there are many partial points of view of the actual world. It is the author's belief, nevertheless, that with enough sight a perceiver is capable of truly comprehending the entire world, however complex it may be. While the "sight" of each character in the book is limited to one or another degree by the circumstances of that character's life, the author has supplied the alert reader with all the information necessary to process the different points of view, and achieve a true and accurate picture of all of reality. Of course this struggle between blindness and sight, truth and darkness, is taking place on the pages of a novel, a creation of the author's own perceptions. Wright would concede that *Native Son* is a fictional representation of reality, but he would also contend, as a naturalist, that it is a true one, conceived in an almost scientific spirit.

It should not surprise us that, in the immediate aftermath of Mary's death, Bigger comes to think he has done something positive. The world he lives in is twisted around. It is a land of plenty where millions starve, a democracy where millions have no rights. Truth for Bigger is twisted around also; Mary's death now elates him, and gives him power over others for the first time in his life. The ever-present knot in his stomach loosens. Though the crime itself was really an accident, Bigger acted when he burned Mary's

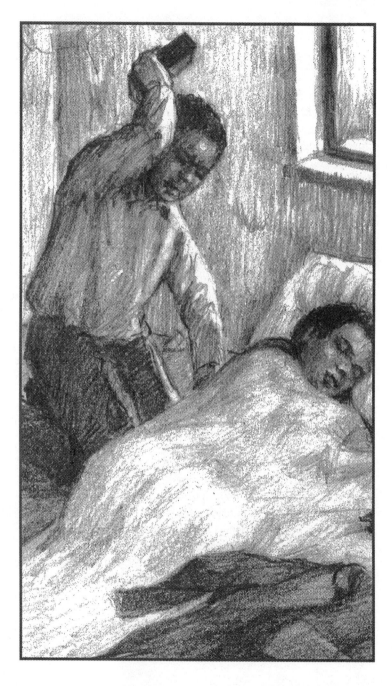

body to cover it up, and he continues to act by manipulating Peggy, and Mr. Britten, and the Dalton family, getting them to believe what he wants them to believe. He especially enjoys turning their hatred of communism to his own advantage, even though in doing so he is hurting those whites— Jan especially—who are closest to him in thinking. In one disturbing passage, Bigger even admires fascist leaders Hitler and Mussolini, for the absolute power they wield over people. He believes that he himself has now had a taste of that power. At certain times the "sight" that is created by Bigger's new sense of power is acute, as when he comes to realize that Mr. Dalton, the apparently generous supporter of Negro education, is in reality a cruel slumlord.

However, the reader can see things that Bigger cannot, and understands that Bigger's "power" is momentary and fleeting. Those who have real power are free to act as they choose, but Bigger, before too long, is everywhere besieged by limiting forces. Bessie is the first to discover the secret of Mary's death, and her awakening to the truth signals the advent of Bigger's return to darkness. He responds by wanting to "blot her out." Whenever Bigger encounters something that limits or controls him, he wants to blot it out, to remove it from his sight. He does blot out Bessie, literally, brutally, in the freezing darkness of an abandoned tenement hideout. There is no freedom, no sight or power in his shocking act, however, only desperation and necessity. Everywhere the world is closing in around him.

Book Two: Flight ends with Bigger's capture by the vigilante mob. Here the reader encounters the heavy symbolism of the cold, white snow, and the huge and looming whiteness of the water tower. Bigger falls from the white tower, lands in the white snow, and looks up to see that he is surrounded by a sea of white faces. They stretch out his arms and step on his wrists, making him sink deeper into the whiteness. It is a whiteness that is also the darkness, the same unrelenting power that has always darkened Bigger's life. He is absolutely not free now, no matter how much insight he gained in the few hours when he felt he was in control of things.

Study Questions

1. What experience causes Bigger to look with disgust at his family's tenement room?

2. What lie does Bigger tell to Mr. and Mrs. Dalton and Mr. Britten, to make them think that Jan must know something about Mary's disappearance?

3. Why does Bigger keep the Communist pamphlets Jan has given him, and what happens when they are discovered?

4. Why does Bessie drink liquor, and what does her drinking have to do with her relationship to Bigger?

5. How does Bessie give Bigger the idea to pretend Mary has been kidnapped, and then to try to extort ransom money from the Daltons?

6. How does Bigger use the ransom note to cast suspicion about Mary's disappearance on the Communists?

7. What does Bigger do that leads to the discovery of Mary's remains, and why does he do it?

8. Who finds Mary's remains, and under what circumstances does he find them?

9. Why does Bigger force Bessie to flee with him, and why does he kill her?

10. What crime besides murder do the whites who are hunting for Bigger assume that he has committed, and why do they assume this? Has Bigger committed this crime?

Answers

1. Bigger is filled with disgust and shame at his family's cramped and dirty room after he has seen the Daltons' magnificent and spacious home.

2. Bigger tells them that he drove both Jan and Mary back to the Dalton house last night, when in fact he had dropped Jan off and returned home with only Mary.

3.   Bigger keeps the pamphlets, because he intends to use them
     to throw more suspicion on Jan. Ultimately, he manages to
     do so, but not before Mr. Britten, who discovers the pam-
     phlets, unexpectedly accuses Bigger of being a Communist.
     Bigger is shaken by the accusation but is able to maintain
     that he did not want the pamphlets and has not read them,
     and that Jan forced him to accept them. Britten and Mr.
     Dalton eventually think what Bigger wants them to think:
     that Jan is a sly communist who has tried to recruit a simple,
     innocent Negro servant.

4.   The sensation Bessie feels when she is drunk is a pleasant
     release from the drudgery of her daily routine of working
     long hours as servant to a white family. She likes Bigger be-
     cause he gives her money for liquor; he likes her because
     she allows him to have sex with her.

5.   Bessie mentions to Bigger that the Daltons live near "Loeb,"
     of "Leopold and Loeb." These were two rich white Chicago
     youths who, seeking to commit the "perfect crime," mur-
     dered another boy in 1924, and tried to make the victim's
     parents pay ransom before the body was found. Both were
     caught and imprisoned.

6.   Bigger signs his note "Red," which is a slang term for "com-
     munist," and also draws the Communist Party's hammer-
     and-sickle emblem (signifying the unity of the workers and
     farmers against the rich capitalists).

7.   Bigger is asked by Peggy to clean out the ash-filled furnace
     at a time when Britten and his men, and many newspaper
     reporters are present in the basement. He is understandably
     afraid to do this, so he just dumps more coal on the already
     low fire, hoping it will burn hotter. Instead, the coal chokes
     the fire, filling the basement with smoke.

8.   Amidst the smoky confusion caused by Bigger's miscalcula-
     tion, an otherwise unidentified newspaper reporter rushes
     to clean out the furnace, and finds a few of Mary's bones,
     and her earring in the ashes.

9. Having fled the Dalton house, Bigger knows that all the police in Chicago will soon be searching for him, and that they will question everyone he knows, including Bessie. With a pitiless and self-serving logic, he forces her to flee with him so that she cannot talk to the police, and then kills her so that he might move from hideout to hideout with greater ease and stealth.

10. The white authorities assume that Bigger raped Mary, and only killed her and burned her body to cover it up. Their assumption reveals that they harbor the crude and deadly racist notion that black men are little more than beasts who cannot resist raping white women. Bigger, of course, did not rape Mary.

Suggested Essay Topics

1. Bigger has killed Mary accidentally, yet he soon convinces himself that what he has done was no accident, and that it was right and natural. He even feels a sense of elation about it. Discuss the reasons that lead him to feel this way.

2. Describe some of the many ways in which Bessie Mears, Bigger's girlfriend, is trapped in a life that is not of her own choosing.

3. Mr. Dalton's private investigator, Mr. Britten, alternately expresses his hatred of African Americans and of Communists. After he interrogates Bigger, he thinks to himself that "Britten was familiar to him; he had met a thousand Brittens in his life." What is it about Britten's thinking that makes him so easy for Bigger to understand, and how does Bigger intend to use Britten's prejudices to his own advantage?

4. Describe the way in which Bigger is hunted down after he has fled the Dalton home. How would this manhunt have been different if Bigger were white?

Book 3: Fate

New Characters:

Boris A. Max: *lawyer from Labor Defenders, a Communist Party group, who takes Bigger's case*

Reverend Hammond: *pastor of Mrs. Thomas' church*

Deputy Coroner: *state investigator who conducts the preliminary inquest of Bigger's case*

Chief Justice Alvin C. Hanley: *the judge who decides Bigger's case*

Mrs. Rawlson: *Mrs. Dalton's mother*

Stenographer: *otherwise unidentified white man who takes down Bigger's jailhouse confession*

H. M. O'Dorsey: *the governor of Illinois*

Calvin H. Robinson: *police psychiatrist*

Summary

All of the action in the novel to this point has taken place during less than two days—a much shorter span of time than it would seem at first glance. In *Fate*, with Bigger in custody and his life hanging in the balance, time appears very short indeed, even though several weeks elapse.

Bigger spends the first few days of his captivity as if he was in a trance. He is brought food but does not eat; he is threatened and bullied, but does not speak. Something inside him has given way. He feels empty, passive, defeated.

He is brought shackled to his pretrial hearing. This inquest is held before a "grand jury", six white men who will decide whether and for what crimes Bigger shall be tried. Bigger notices Mr. and Mrs. Dalton and Jan Erlone among the faces he sees there. He faints, mainly from hunger and thirst, and when he is revived, he is back in his cell.

Bigger now takes a renewed interest in his fate. He eats and drinks, and asks for a newspaper, where he finds another lurid, racist story about himself. Bigger falls asleep but is soon awakened by a visitor. He is Reverend Hammond, pastor of Mrs. Thomas' church, who preaches to Bigger, and then reads aloud a long passage from *Genesis* in the Bible. He hangs a wooden cross around Bigger's neck just as Jan enters the cell. In a moving speech, Jan explains that when he found out that Bigger had killed his girlfried, he at first wanted to kill Bigger. Now, however, he wants desperately to put an end to the hatred, and to understand Bigger, and help him if he can. Bigger is moved by Jan's sincerity, but tells him that his case is hopeless. Over the protestations of Reverend Hammond, who believes redemption is only attained after death, Jan brings in Boris A. Max, the Jewish lawyer from Labor Defenders. Quickly, Max persuades Bigger to accept his counsel. Then David A. Buckley, the state's attorney, comes into the cell. He is surprised to see Max there, and tries to dissuade him from taking the case, telling him that the state has all the evidence it needs to send Bigger to the electric chair, with or without Max's defense. Max does not budge from his support of Bigger. Buckley then brings in Mr. and Mrs. Dalton to buttress his arguments. He contends that Max should help the Daltons, who are supportive of "Negroes" generally, rather than a killer like Bigger. Mr. Dalton asks Bigger for the name of his accomplice, convinced that Bigger alone could never have committed such an elaborate crime. Then Bigger's mother, brother, and sister are brought into the cell, and, behind them, Gus, G.H., and Jack, his friends from the poolroom. Bigger feels ashamed for his terror-stricken family, and is pained by their helpless and subservient position. He learns that his three friends were arrested, but that Jan and Boris Max got them out of jail. The entire fantastic scene—there are now thirteen people in Bigger's cell—culminates when Mrs. Thomas, sobbing, falls to her knees and begs the Daltons to spare Bigger's life. In her plea, we learn that she has been evicted from her tenement, which the Daltons own. The Daltons agree to allow the Thomases to stay where they are, but say they can do nothing for Bigger. The pathetic scene paralyzes Bigger with shame.

All leave the cell except Buckley. He tells Bigger that the Communists do not want to help him, but only want to exploit his case for their own gain. He says that they will prolong Bigger's agony, and that the longer the trial goes on, the more difficult it will be for the state to prevent the lynch mob that has gathered outside from

breaking into the prison and killing Bigger. Buckley dramatically opens a window, so that Bigger can hear the hysterical taunts of the white mob. Buckley wants him to sign a confession. He wants to know if Jan had been involved in Mary's death. Buckley also reveals that the police have found Bessie's body, and he tells Bigger that she did not die right away, but froze to death struggling to get out of the airshaft. Buckley also knows that Bigger raped Bessie. He then begins to accuse Bigger of many other, unsolved crimes, especially rapes, and claims that two women identified him as their attacker while he was passed out in his cell. Bigger, who has been silent, denies these false charges, and he refuses to implicate Jan, despite Buckley's insistence that it was Jan who must have written the ransom note. Buckley hammers away at Bigger, claiming his case is lost, and revealing that the state knows much about his recent activities. They know that he and his friends planned to rob Blum's delicatessen, and even that he and Jack masturbated in the movie theater. Worn out, Bigger confesses. A stenographer takes down his every word, and Bigger signs the paper.

Shortly thereafter Bigger is once again taken in chains to the inquest. On the way, he is attacked by a hissing mob. Inside the room, amidst a "solid sheet of white faces", he sees all the evidence laid out on a table, including Mary's bones, his ransom note, and his signed confession. Max is there and reassures Bigger that he will not have to speak.

The deputy coroner politely questions Mrs. Dalton, implying in his questions that Mary had been raped. He then belligerently questions Jan Erlone, accusing him of getting Mary drunk, and then offering her to Bigger, as a way of recruiting him to the Communist Party. He invents wild theories about Jan, including one holding that Jan himself wanted to have sex with Bigger. Bigger sees that the same men who hate him also hate Jan, and he sympathizes with Jan. Mr. Dalton is next to be called. Boris Max questions him, and effectively discloses how Dalton perpetuates and profits from the segregation of African Americans into substandard housing that he controls. The deputy coroner then calls for Bigger, but Max objects, and Bigger does not have to testify.

The inquest closes when the deputy coroner, to Bigger's horror and over Max's vociferous objections, brings in the battered remains

of Bessie Mears for the grand jury to examine. The jury retires, and soon returns charges of murder and rape against Bigger.

In a macabre scene, Bigger is taken through a taunting mob to a police car, which brings him to the Dalton home. He is then taken out of the car, through another mob, and brought upstairs to Mary's room. The police demand that Bigger reenact his rape of Mary, in the presence of newspaper photographers. Bigger is terrified but stands up to them, and refuses. He is then dragged back outside, where the mob awaits, and where a huge cross has been set aflame, the symbol of Ku Klux Klan terror.

Bigger is taken to a new jail, and there he angrily confronts Reverend Hammond, who has come for another visit. Bigger throws down his wooden cross, and shoves back the opening cell door, sending the preacher sprawling. The guard tells Hammond that the Communists must be responsible for Bigger's new hatred of the cross. Shaken, Hammond departs.

Afterwards, Bigger reads in a newspaper that he will probably be executed, and that Buckley has said that the Communists are at the bottom of this and many other such crimes. A supposedly insane black man is briefly brought into Bigger's cell, but there is much truth in his excited ravings about racism. Bigger notices that even jails are racially segregated. Max comes to visit him again. Bigger trusts him now, because he knows Max has incurred the hatred of all the racists for defending him. For the first time in his life, Bigger opens up to another person, and gives voice to his private thoughts. He at last tells his side of the story, even admitting that, though he did not rape Mary, the two had felt an alcohol-induced mutual attraction. He explains to Max the hopelessness of being black in a country run by white racists. He wanted to be an aviator once, but what chance did he have, when blacks were not allowed to acquire such specialized training? He is only allowed to sweep streets or shine shoes, and then go to church on Sunday, to be told that everything will be fine in heaven, when he is dead. He admits to Max that he, for one, could not accept that kind of life. He had to live differently, and he supposes now that his rebelliousness led him to kill. He is not sorry for what he has done. Max only tries to point out that there are some blacks, and whites, too, whose rebelliousness has found a creative expression, in the struggle to make a new world, and he suggests that Bigger might have sought them out. Max departs, and there is a new warmth between lawyer and client. Bigger, who to this point has been resigned to his fate, now experiences a new understanding, and is suddenly and tragically filled with a powerful will to live.

Bigger reads in the papers that the governor of Illinois has called out the National Guard to keep peace during his trial. He also reads of the "scientific"—and crudely racist—explanations that prominent psychologists are offering for his actions.

Finally, the trial begins. The authorities, with the aid of the press, have stirred a mountain of white hatred against Bigger. Since a jury would be all-white, Max has decided to allow the judge alone to adjudicate Bigger's case. Max is hoping, not for an aquittal of course, but only that Bigger's life be spared, and that he be allowed to spend the rest of it in jail. Buckley, who is prosecuting the case, tries to intimidate the judge by again opening a window, letting in the sounds of the screaming mob outside. When he eventually proceeds, Buckley reveals that he has sixty witnesses. Max objects that all these witnesses are unnecessary, because Bigger has already pleaded guilty. The judge nevertheless allows all of them to be called. Buckley, who is running for re-election, presents his extravagant, showy case. Fifteen newspaper reporters, sixteen policemen, and an array of doctors and fingerprint experts appear. Even the owner of the Regal Theater is called up to testify that Jack and Bigger masturbated there. Twelve workmen bring in the pieces of the Daltons' furnace and reassemble it in the courtroom. Buckley has a white girl of Mary's size crawl into it, to show how Bigger cut off Mary's head. However, when Buckley calls Jan Erlone, he no longer tries to link him to Bigger's crimes.

Max does not cross-examine any of the state's witnesses. He knows that Bigger will be convicted of murdering Mary and Bessie. His entire defense will be his closing statement, his plea for Bigger's life. Max's speech is much more than a legal argument, however. It is a complete and unambiguous—though complex—description and assessment of the root causes of Bigger's actions.

He immediately sets Bigger's crime in a larger context. He mentions how the authorities used the hunt for Bigger as an excuse to terrorize the entire African-American population, to break

into the offices of the Communist Party, and to raid labor unions and other worker organizations. Max links this campaign of police terror to Buckley's election promise to the rich citizens of Chicago that he will forcibly end all strikes and mass demonstrations by the poor. The outrage against Bigger's crimes have been cynically amplified, says Max, who points out that gangsters often commit gruesome murders, are quietly jailed, and soon freed to kill again. He goes on to sketch the entire world into which Bigger was born, and which created him and governed his actions. It is a world of plenty, which excites the senses, but then denies fulfillment to entire sections of its inhabitants. Bigger might have made something of himself. He even wanted to do so, but all the higher paths of human endeavor are blocked to African Americans. For Bigger there was no escape from the ghetto pressure-cooker, and he lived the only way he could. Max even remarks that a second civil war may result in this country if the white authorities continue to treat its twelve million African Americans (the 1930s population) like animals rather than human beings. Max does not attempt to justify Bigger's actions. He only asks that they be understood, in this greater context. He asks that Bigger be allowed to live, albeit in prison. Max says that such an act of clemency on the part of the authorities, made in the midst of the howling cries for more blood, would allow for the possibility of growth, of understanding, both for Bigger, and for those who would kill him.

Bigger does not understand Max's long speech, but he is proud that Max made it for him. After a brief recess, the prosecutor Buckley makes his closing remarks. His speech is full of stock phrases about law and order, but also of jarring racist references to Bigger as a "half-human black ape" and a "mad black dog." He says that "every decent white man in America" should be joyful "for the opportunity to crush with his heel the wooly head of this black lizard." He again stresses that Bigger's central crime is rape—not of Bessie, of course, who was black, but of Mary, the white woman. Buckley closes with a blood-curdling demand that Bigger Thomas die for his crimes. One hour later, the judge comes back with his decision: Bigger will die.

Back in a cell for his final days, Bigger broods over his awful fate, and refuses all visitors except one: Max. He is still grateful to

Max for his closing speech at the trial. Furthermore, their earlier, prolonged talk remains very important to Bigger. Max has tried to appeal to the governor for clemency, but his appeal is denied. He arrives at Bigger's cell a few hours before he is to be electrocuted. Bigger desperately wants to talk as they talked before, but finds it difficult to speak, because time is short. When he does speak, he stutters from anxiety. Movingly, Bigger assures Max that he is satisfied that Max has done everything he could to save him. In the discussion that ensues, Bigger is hungry for more understanding. He tells Max that he never wanted to kill, something that Max already knows. At first, Bigger's deathhouse intensity frightens Max. With difficulty, he tells Bigger that he should die free of the guilt that others have put on him. He says to Bigger that he is not alone, that the capitalist class has deprived millions of their rightful future. He also says that in the struggle between the capitalists and those they oppress, the side with the most humanity will win. That is why Bigger must believe in himself, and not in the system that oppresses him and those like him. Bigger tells Max that he does believe in himself. For Bigger, however, believing in himself is also believing in his crimes, which he now regards as his life's only meaningful actions. He tells Max that the killings define him, and that "what I killed for must've been good!" Max backs away in horror at what Bigger is saying, but Bigger is firm. It is all the understanding he has time for. He tells Max that he is all right, and asks that he greet his mother and Jan for him. Max cries at the end, but Bigger does not, will not. Instead, as Max leaves, he smiles a little.

Analysis

When *Native Son* first appeared, some African-American leaders recoiled at Wright's portrait of Bigger Thomas. They felt that by making Bigger the perpetrator of brutal crimes, Wright undermined the novel's message about racism, and gave white racists another target at which to aim their hatred. Wright was unmoved by these arguments, and believed that those who made them misunderstand not only his novel, but the complex world in which we all live. Wright knew of course that not all young African-American men who live in northern ghettos turn out like Bigger. Wright's own

early experiences in fact had much in common with Bigger's. However, Wright was acutely aware that ghetto life was producing far too many Bigger Thomases. Oppression, Wright would say, oppresses. Apart from the crimes he commits, the varieties of outward behavior which Bigger displays are actually common ones for many ghetto dwellers. Bigger is alternately sullen and brutish toward his family and other African Americans, and he is fearful and servile before whites. Just as the society is split, so is Bigger's outward behavior, and he is not permitted to develop an integrated, healthy personality. Inwardly, he is tied up in a knot of fear and anger, and is occasionally driven to distraction by powerful but ill-defined desires. Bigger is a human being, with all the potential in him for human growth, but is everywhere denied opportunity. For Richard Wright, it would have been a dishonest fantasy to create a wholly appealing and angelic Bigger Thomas. Instead of denying reality, therefore, the author plunged into it without reservation, and brought back an unsettling and sometimes shocking tale, so that readers might see precisely how racism and poverty deform living human beings.

When he wrote *Native Son*, Richard Wright believed firmly that racism and poverty could only be wiped out by another American revolution, made by the suffering masses, black and white alike. He felt that moderate solutions—reforms—were not solutions at all, because they would leave intact the underlying mechanism that created racism and poverty: the capitalist system. In *Fate*, the novel's final section, the existing, oppressive world collides vividly with the author's hopeful vision for the future. Within this essential clash, Bigger's own, personal point of view begins—but only begins—to grow in a new direction.

The old, existing world is far more tangible, far more present, than the world that is arising to oppose it. The old world's mouthpiece is David Buckley, Bigger's prosecutor. His argument at Bigger's trial is simple, apparently: Bigger has committed capital crimes; he must be put to death. However, the underpinning of his "simple" argument is not so simple. Buckley is attempting to get re-elected, and part of his campaign strategy is to use Bigger to whip up race hysteria in whites, and then to portray himself as the protector of the white race, his constituency. The press is his willing tool, and

Chicago's newspapers dutifully record Buckley's cynical manipulations, casting them as moral outrage. Furthermore, the reader learns that Buckley has promised the "Loop bankers" (the "Loop" is Chicago's central business district) and the "Manufacturers' Association" that if re-elected, he will crack down on the then prevalent struggles of the needy, such as strikes and pro-welfare demonstrations. In accord with his promise, Buckley uses the hunt for Bigger as an excuse to make police raids not only on African-American homes, but also on the organizations of the workers and the poor. Buckley wants to electrocute Bigger Thomas for reasons, therefore, other than moral outrage or a desire for justice. The racist hysteria, the police terror of the manhunt, Bigger's showy trial and his ultimate execution—all strengthen the rule of Buckley and his wealthy backers.

Buckley serves as spokesman for the old, race and class-divided world, but that the world is everywhere in the novel. It is the Thomas family's rat-infested home, and the Dalton's mansion; it is Doc's poolroom, and the Florida resort where Mary Dalton cavorted. It is Mr. Dalton's wealth, and the figures and institutions of authority that surround and protect it from its rightful owners. It is a courtroom ringed by a screaming white mob, where a young black man sits, waiting to be condemned.

Wright's new world is not yet born; it exists only potentially. Boris Max, Bigger's lawyer is an advocate of this world, and into his mouth the author has put his own analysis of the present, and description of the future. Max's plea for Bigger's life is long, and Wright cut out much of it from the first edition of the novel, at the request of his publisher. Now that it is restored to the text in its original form, the reader can enjoy the partisan overview that the author intended to be present at the end of the novel. Max not only negates with withering criticism the "law-and-order" world of the Buckleys and the Daltons, but he also presents a positive progam for the future, wherein all the alienated and desperate Bigger Thomases, black and white, will be able to explore their full, human potentials. He tears away all the veils limiting each individual point of view, and the reader might now gaze upon the world as a great and complex struggle between oppressor and oppressed. It was the author's sincere hope, as an African American, and also as a

Communist, that a way be found to draw the Bigger Thomases into this struggle in a conscious way, so that their violent or servile lives might be turned onto a creative path.

Max's speech, while a necessary part of the trial, is also abstracted from the action. It is a set-piece of universal political and social philosophy that on its own cannot and does not alter the trial's outcome. Without it, the novel's ultimate message would have been difficult to decipher, but it also runs far ahead of Bigger's own understanding and development. In *Fate*, Bigger does in fact search for understanding, and he is inspired to do so by his contact with Boris Max. This is not Max the abstract speechmaker, but Max the human being. For a work of art such as a novel to succeed, it is very important that it bring abstract, universal truth down to a subjective level, so that it can develop organically, within a living human being. The reader can see such a development of true insight in Bigger at various points in the novel, but nowhere so dramatically as in his first, prolonged jailhouse conversation with Max. There he begins to speak for himself, to tell his own story for the first time. He speaks haltingly, and up against the limits of his education and background, but he does speak. He at last chooses his own words, and not the words he thinks others want to hear. He voices his own feelings as an individual, but he also begins to feel himself as part of a larger whole. He feels sympathy toward Max and toward Jan, because he sees that they too have somehow fallen afoul of the same white power structure that has oppressed him. Bigger speaks with insistence and sincerity. His is a true voice; though he is still afraid, he does not mask his thoughts in his customarily brutish or servile manner.

When Max and Bigger meet for the last time, Bigger has been condemned to die and has only hours to live. Bigger is anxious to pick up where they left off, but for Max, there is defeat and desperation in the air. He tries to reach out to Bigger, but he can only speak with difficulty. Furthermore, when Bigger speaks, Max is shocked by what he says. Even Max, whose active sympathy for African-American struggles is strong, has only partial "sight." He has not had to live Bigger's life, and he does not have to die as Bigger will die. Bigger recalls the feeling of power he had after he killed. In the hour of death, he finds he must embrace the killings as his life's only meaningful actions, even if he did not want to kill. "What I killed for must've been good!...I feel all right when I look at it that way," he tells Max. Bigger's summary thoughts are indeed shocking, and Max reacts to them with terror. Bigger, however, is at ease with these thoughts. He has found a way to face death.

Although Bigger's understanding had begun to develop, it cannot proceed. It is stunted by the fact of his impending execution, his fate. The only life Bigger Thomas ever knew was filled with horrors, great and small. Therefore, his first ideas, his first self-evaluation, his first conscious expression of morality—these must reflect those horrors, embody them. He will live no other life, nor will he think other thoughts; he has no more time. In these ways, Bigger's limited growth is still a part of his past. Yet we can also see another Bigger, one who is not so horrifying, who does not shock us. We see this Bigger in the sincerity he displays toward Max, and in his final, cheerful greeting to Jan that he wants Max to convey. We only just glimpse this other Bigger, because he is the Bigger of the future, and the future has been denied to him. He is the Bigger who might have been an aviator.

Study Questions

1. What is the difference between a grand jury and a trial jury? Between an inquest and a trial?

2. Shortly after Bigger recovers from his fainting spell at the inquest, twelve people come to see him in his cell. Who are they?

3. What are some of the reasons that Bigger begins to trust Jan and Boris Max?

4. Why does Bigger attack Reverend Hammond and discard the cross Hammond has given him?

5. What two incidents in the novel indicate that the author believes that the psychiatric profession has contributed to racism?

6. Why does Boris Max, Bigger's lawyer, ask that the judge alone, and not a trial jury, decide Bigger's fate?

7. What plea does Max enter on Bigger's behalf, and why does he do so?

8. How many witnesses does prosecutor Buckley call to testify against Bigger? Why does Max object to his calling so many?

9. What charge against Bigger is most important to prosecutor Buckley? Why?

10. In their last meeting, what does Bigger say that so disturbs Boris Max?

Answers

1. A grand jury is convened to decide whether and on what charges an accused person should be indicted and tried. The grand jury hearing is also known as an inquest. If a grand jury recommends an indictment, then a trial may follow, at which a trial jury (or petit jury) is asked to render a verdict— to decide whether the accused person is or is not guilty. The accused also has the right to request that the judge alone, and not a trial jury, render a verdict.

2. Visiting Bigger are Reverend Hammond, Jan Erlone, Boris Max, David Buckley (the prosecutor), Mr. and Mrs. Dalton, Mrs. Thomas, Vera and Buddy Thomas, Gus, G.H., and Jack Harding.

3. Although Bigger believes that Jan and Max do not fully understand how he feels, he begins to trust them. He sees that Jan has lost someone he has loved, and even though Bigger is responsible for his loss, Jan, instead of hating Bigger, wants to understand him. Moreover, Bigger knows that many whites who hate him, also hate Jan and Max, because they are Communists. Finally, though Bigger does not understand Max's speech at the trial, he recognizes that Max made it on his behalf and is proud of it on this basis.

4. The immediate cause of Bigger's hostility for Reverend Hammond and the cross arises out of his awful encounter, outside the Dalton home, with a flaming cross, the symbol of Ku Klux Klan terror against African Americans. However,

as Bigger later tells Max, he has always felt that religion served to keep African Americans submissive, because justice, according to the prevailing religious notion, comes only in the afterlife. "I want to be happy in this world, not out of it," he says.

5. Wright expresses his disdain for the racism of the psychiatric profession in the episode when a black man who is considered insane by the white authorities is put into Bigger's cell. The man may well be disturbed, but his "ravings" about racism are fundamentally true. In a second instance of psychiatric racism, Bigger reads an article about his case in which psychologists pronounce African-American men unable to resist white women.

6. If a jury were convened for Bigger's trial, it would have been all-white, just like the grand jury was. Racism has tainted every professedly democratic institution in America, at one time or another. In the judicial system, African Americans have often been excluded from juries, especially when the accused was also African American. Given the racist climate in which the trial is being conducted, Max believes that Bigger has a better chance of getting a life sentence (as opposed to a death sentence) from the judge than from an all-white jury.

7. Max enters a plea of "guilty" for Bigger. Because of the overwhelming evidence against Bigger, including his own signed confession, Max knows that the judge will find him guilty, no matter what his defense might be. He decides to confine himself to trying to save Bigger from the electric chair, so that he might spend the rest of his life in prison.

8. Buckley calls sixty witnesses. Max objects that these are too many, because Bigger has already pleaded guilty. Max feels that the witnesses will only serve to excite race hate against African Americans, which, of course, is Buckley's intention.

9. Buckley especially focuses on the charge that Bigger has raped Mary Dalton. Although the charge is untrue, it is the most racially inflammatory. Buckley is running for re-election to another term as Illinois state's attorney, and part

of his campaign strategy involves exciting racial hatred in whites.

10. In an attempt to find a meaning in his life and his actions, and to find a way to face death, Bigger tells Max that he must have had a good and worthy reason to kill, a reason he must have believed in very deeply. He also says that he did not feel alive in this world until he "felt things hard enough kill for 'em." He concludes by telling Max, "I'm all right. I feel all right when I look at it that way."

Suggested Essay Topics

1. To further serve the realism of his novel, the author has adapted many actual articles about a real case similar to Bigger's, which appeared in Chicago newspapers. What is most noticeable about these articles, and by including them, what is the author saying about the role of the press in American society?

2. In a long and dramatic scene, a total of twelve people are brought into Bigger's cell. In "How 'Bigger' Was Born," Richard Wright admitted that this scene was not strictly realistic. Discuss the scene, and how it serves the novel's artistic aims, despite its being physically improbable.

3. In light of his confrontation with Reverend Hammond, and his conversation with Boris Max, discuss Bigger's attitude toward Christianity. How do Bigger's views compare with those of his mother's and of Jan Erlone's?

4. In *Book Three: Fate*, Bigger has two very important conversations with Boris Max. Describe what these conversations mean to Bigger, and suggest an explanation for the final, disturbing thoughts he expresses to Max about his crimes.

How "Bigger" Was Born

Summary and Analysis:

Native Son was published by Harper & Brothers on March 1, 1940. On March 12 of the same year, Richard Wright delivered the lecture, "How 'Bigger' Was Born," at Columbia University in New York City. He eventually gave this lecture four more times, twice in Harlem, and in Chicago and North Carolina. Harper's soon published the lecture as a pamphlet, and it was included in subsequent editions of the novel. It is also included in the restored text of *Native Son*, published by The Library of America in 1991, and HarperPerennial in 1993.

Unlike some artists, who feel strongly that once they have created a work of art, their job is done, Wright was eager to discuss and explain the significance of his creation. He concedes that there are "meanings in my book of which I was not aware until they literally spilled out upon the paper." Nevertheless, he makes an effort to describe those meanings which he did put consciously into *Native Son*. Therefore, for those readers who value an author's intentions (and there are many these days who do not), and who believe that successful literature is in the main a conscious creation, "How 'Bigger' Was Born" is a document of great import, a gift.

As was partly discussed in the analysis of *Book One: Fear*, Wright identifies in his lecture several sources from his own experience that led him to create the fictional Bigger Thomas. The first source was his youthful encounters with five separate real-life

Bigger Thomases, who lived in the South. "Bigger No. 1" was a childhood bully, who taunted Wright and his friends; "Bigger No. 2" was
a teen-aged boy who did not disguise his contempt for white-run
society. He bought things on credit at white-owned stores and never
paid for them; he lived in white-owned shacks and did not pay rent.
Wright tells us that the last he heard of "Bigger No. 2," he was in
prison. When Wright worked as a ticket-taker in a Negro movie
house, he encountered "Bigger No. 3," who routinely gave him a
painful pinch and pushed past him without paying. Bigger No. 3,
we learn, was later shot in the back and killed by a white cop while
delivering liquor during prohibition. "Bigger No. 4" was another
rebel who broke the "Jim Crow" segregation laws—remember, before the civil rights movement of the 1950s and 1960s, African
Americans were forcibly, legally separated from white society in
the South. Bigger No. 4 often stated the simple truth that "white
folks won't let us do nothing." He was ultimately declared insane
and put in a mental institution. "Bigger No. 5" defiantly refused,
knife in hand, to sit in the "colored" section on streetcars—an action that had potentially deadly consequences. Wright remarks, "I
don't know what happened to Bigger No. 5. But I can guess." What
was unique about each of these Biggers was not their poverty or
their want of basic human rights. All African Americans existed
under these conditions. It was their defiance that set the Biggers
apart. It was not an organized, consciously political defiance; it was
elemental, often brutal, and dangerous.

Another source Wright drew upon when he created Bigger was
a job he once had in Chicago's South Side Boys' Club. The club was
funded by rich whites who ostensibly wanted to help ghettoized
black youth. Wright was employed as a kind of recreation counse-
lor, and organized games of ping-pong, marbles, checkers, and
baseball. He points out that funding the club was not an act of
charity on the part of its wealthy patrons: its real purpose was to
distract these teens and keep them off the streets, where they might
steal or otherwise harm the "valuable white property which ad-
joined the Black Belt" ghetto. Wright admits that he hoped the
youths, these wronged and angry Bigger Thomases, would go out
and steal anyway, and prove how ridiculous—even obscene—it was
to think that the effects of ghetto existence could be improved by

ping-pong. He reveals that his hopes were usually satisfied. (This episode from Wright's life offers a good example of how closely the details in *Native Son* adhere to reality. In the novel, it is revealed that one of Mr. Dalton's charitable deeds was to donate ping-pong tables to a center for black youth.)

Wright found yet another source of inspiration for *Native Son* in the white public's reaction to his previous book, *Uncle Tom's Children.* That collection of stories about the terror of *Southern* racism provoked much sympathy from Northern liberals. "I had written a book," Wright laments, "that even bankers' daughters could read and weep over and feel good about." He made a vow to himself that his next book "would be so hard and deep that they would have to face it without the consolation of tears." His earlier book exposed with rare and almost pictoral accuracy the horrors of Southern racism, and thus it drew the unwanted sympathy even of wealthy Northern whites, the oppressors and ghettoizers of Northern blacks. In *Native Son*, Wright remedied his oversight, by setting his story in Chicago, and by drawing the stark line that existed between ghetto dwellers like the Thomases, and wealthy (and possibly liberal) whites like the Daltons. Wright also insured his book against the unwelcome sympathies of "bankers' daughters" by creating Bigger Thomas—a character without hope, brutalized by ghetto life, who harbors an elemental hate for a world he understands only imperfectly.

Wright's explanation of his sources of inspiration reveal that he believes Bigger Thomas represents a genuine type of African American, one who has been ignored in literature. The reasons that a certain percentage of African Americans should have become dangerous rebels are not hard to grasp. For those who are naive enough to be shocked by the actions of the Bigger Thomases of the world, Wright briefly surveys the history of white rule in the South after slavery. Despite the promise of "radical reconstruction"—a political program designed and advocated by white abolitionists and African American leaders such as Frederick Douglass—the freed slaves faced a new kind of slavery in the postwar South. Above all, radical reconstruction called for granting African-American men the right to vote (all women were barred from voting in the United States until 1920—Southern black women were not permitted to vote until 1965). It also advocated African-American education, that former slaves be granted lands to till, and that their rights be protected against the former slave-owning class by the continued presence in the South of thousands of Union soldiers. Radical reconstruction was eventually defeated however, by political chicanery and outright terror. Union troops were withdrawn from the South, and the unofficial military arm of the former slave-owners—the Ku Klux Klan—imposed a sub-human status on African Americans, through depraved acts of torture, individual lynchings, and mass executions. As Wright remarks, millions of Negroes were deprived of land, of the ballot, and of the right to use public places. More than this, African Americans were also deprived of the right to an education. As Bigger No. 4, whom white society declared insane, used to say, "white folks won't let us do nothing." (At the time, Wright was speaking, it would still be 25 years before Southern blacks would win their struggle for basic legal rights.)

Blacks were thus forcibly prevented from enjoying the riches of the world around them, which through their labor they had helped to create. Yet, African-American communities in the South, no more than shantytowns, lay side-by-side with more affluent white areas. The sense of alienation that Blacks felt—and still feel in the North as well as the South—was stark and powerful. Prosperity is so close to those who do not prosper, but the way to it is barred, whether by racial laws (in the South), or by economic laws (in the North), and those laws in turn are enforced, ultimately, by the police, the National Guard, and the army.

It is no wonder, then, that Bigger Thomases should emerge. Uneducated, yet fiercely aware of their enforced deprivation, these rebels develop an irrational hatred of everything white. Wright was very much interested in the Bigger Thomas phenomenon, and he actively sought to discover if the alienation that created Bigger was limited to African Americans. Wright's search had important literary and philosophical-political implications for the writer. It led him to treat the theme of alienation often in his literary works, but it also led him away, initially, from African-American centered philosophies, and toward Marxism, which is a general theory of oppression and alienation. In Marx's theory, the essential form of alienation is the alienation of all laborers, white and black, male and female, from the fruits of their labor. This theory appealed to the young Richard Wright, because it held the promise that Black people would not have to stand alone in their struggle against a vast ocean of whiteness. In the Marxist view, society is divided into classes, which are determined by the relationship of people to the means of production of wealth. There are workers, who must sell their own labor power in order to survive, and there are employers, who already have enough material wealth to survive, plus enough left over to buy machinery and buildings, and to employ others (at the lowest possible wage). By exploiting the productivity of their workers, the employing classes are able to become even wealthier. The workers, however, remain workers, and live from paycheck to paycheck. Furthermore, Marx granted that some categories of workers—such as African Americans—were more exploited than others, but he insisted that workers of all countries, all nationalities, all races, had potentially more uniting them than dividing them. The Communist Party of the United States, which espoused the Marxist philosophy, at least on paper, held that black and white workers must unite to conquer racism and class exploitation.

The struggles of labor began to hold Wright's interest. He also found, in stories of the Russian revolutionists, evidence of the more universal form of alienation recognized by Marxism. In his lecture, he cites an important example of one of these stories, which, apart from its message about alienation, sheds light on Wright's difficult relationship with the Communist Party. Because of its double-message, it is useful to examine Wright's example in detail. He tells of "reading (p. 517) an interesting pamphlet telling of the friendship of Gorky and Lenin in exile. The booklet told of how Lenin and Gorky were walking down a London street. Lenin turned to Gorky and, pointing, said: "Here is *their* Big Ben." "There is *their* Westminster Abbey." "There is *their* library."

Vladimir Ilyich Lenin was the leader of the Bolshevik (later, Communist) Party, an illegal party struggling against the tyranny of the Russian czar, who was an absolute monarch. In October 1917, Lenin would lead a revolution in Russia whose aim was to establish a socialist society there. Because all political opposition in

Russia was outlawed, Lenin often lived abroad, to avoid arrest by the czarist police. Maxim Gorky was a famous Russian writer who knew Lenin, and was sympathetic to the revolutionary cause. Wright remarks that Lenin's attitude was one of "exclusion," or alienation from the London landmarks he was pointing out. The landmarks, as magnificent as may be, are the property of the rich, of them, those against whom Lenin and all communists were struggling, in the name of the poorer classes. The landmarks are symbols of an entire, advanced society, a society that was built by the laboring hands of masses of poor people, who are then excluded from enjoying its advantages. Here Wright remarks of Lenin's standpoint, "That's Bigger. That's the Bigger Thomas reaction."

Lenin's attitude in fact helped inspire Wright to become a Communist, but he joined the Communist Party about ten years after Lenin's death, when his successor in Russia, Josef Stalin, and Stalin's faction in the Communist Parties throughout the world, had obtained absolute control. The philosophical position of the Stalinists contained some serious departures from the Marxist idea, and, moreover, Stalin abolished inner-party debate and disagreement, something that Lenin looked upon as valuable and necessary. Richard Wright, during his tenure in the Communist Party of the United States, clashed early and often with the Stalinist regime that ruled it, clashes that led to not only his departure from the Party in 1942, but also to his rejection of Marxism entirely.

In 1940, when he delivered "How 'Bigger' Was Born," Wright was still very much a Party member, though he had already had a series of clashes with the leadership. Nevertheless, he did try to keep to the Party line, and avoided inflaming his difficult situation. Wright's story of Lenin reveals something about his stormy political life. In the opinion of this writer, Richard Wright was well aware that Lenin had no such conversation with Maxim Gorky in exile. In fact, the conversation did occur, in the year 1902, but it took place between Lenin and the second most important leader of the Russian Revolution, Leon Trotsky. After Lenin's death, however, Trotsky struggled against Stalin's political direction, and so became Stalin's mortal enemy. He was expelled first from the Communist Party, and then from the Soviet Union, and, later in the very year that *Native Son* was published, he was assassinated

by Stalin's agent while living in exile in Mexico. It was Trotsky who
first recounted his now-famous London walk with Lenin in an
essay called "Lenin and the Old Iskra," which he included in a
book about Lenin published in 1924 in Moscow. That book was
first translated into English in 1925, and is clearly the work to
which Richard Wright is referring:

> "I no longer remember whether it was this morning or
> another day that I took a long walk with Vladimir Ilyich [Lenin]
> through London. He showed me Westminster Abbey (from
> outside) and some other famous buildings. I no longer know
> how he expressed himself but the meaning was: that this is
> "*their* famous Westminster." The "their" meant, naturally, not
> the English, but the enemy. Not emphatic at all, rather deeply
> organic and revealed by the pitch of his voice, this meaning
> was always obvious when he spoke of any kind of cultural
> values or new conquests, whether it were about the edifica-
> tion of the British Museum or the richness of information of
> the [London] *Times* or, many years later, German artillery or
> French aviation: *They* understand or *they* have, *they* have ac-
> complished or succeeded—but always as enemies! The in-
> visible shadow of the shareholders of society lay, as it were,
> in his eyes on all human culture, and this shadow he felt as
> incontestably as the daylight." (*Lenin*, by Leon Trotsky, New
> York: Capricorn Books, 1962, pp. 7-8).

As the notes for *Native Son* that he left behind reveal, Richard
Wright was a precise researcher and scholar, and he made every
effort in his novel to reproduce the Depression-era Chicago ghetto
as closely as possible. His departures from realism are deliberate,
such as in the scene in *Fate*, where, for dramatic reasons, he brings
twelve visitors into Bigger's small prison cell. It is therefore difficult to imagine that Wright merely "forgot" that the book he had
been reading about Lenin was by Trotsky, or that he accidentally
substituted the name of Gorky for the name of the real author.
Furthermore, Wright was a leading Party intellectual at a time when
every worker involved in the American Communist movement
knew the difference between Trotsky and Gorky. The truth is simply this: Wright did not want to reveal, in a public speech, that a
book of Trotsky's had inspired him, even if the object of that book

was to praise Lenin. Lenin was safely dead, and Stalin, even as he proceeded to arrest and shoot almost all of Lenin's important collaborators, had made the dead Lenin into an almost godlike figure. Trotsky, who was not dead yet, was calling Stalin the betrayer of the revolution, and was ceaselessly exposing his often monstrous lies. Trotsky, therefore, though he had been Lenin's closest ally, was branded by Stalin a "counterrevolutionary," a fascist, an agent of reactionary foreign governments, and the supreme enemy of the Soviet state. A favorable reference to Trotsky or Trotskyism by a member of any Communist Party was grounds for immediate, summary expulsion, a fact of which Wright was well aware.

The narrow dogmatism of the Stalin faction repelled Wright, but in 1940, he was not prepared to break completely with the Communist Party. His attitude in this respect was not an atypical one. Stalinism repelled and confused many thousands who were dedicated to the socialist cause in the 1930s and 1940s. However, because Stalin was the leader of the Soviet Union—the only country in the world that had abolished capitalism—these socialists were reluctant to abandon the Stalinized Communist Parties. The Trotskyist parties, which represented the only revolutionary opposition to Stalinism, were small in comparision, and apparently unviable to most doubting Stalinists. More precisely, Stalin's anti-Trotsky propaganda had infected the thinking of even the most critical Stalinists. And so Richard Wright, like so many of his comrades in the Communist Party, tried to rationalize the Party's policies for as long as he could endure. Then, when he finally did break with the Party, he also broke with revolutionary socialism altogether.

Wright's political problem with the Communist Party, therefore, became a philosophical problem with Marxism. "How 'Bigger' Was Born" not only reflects Wright's problem inadvertently, as in his story of Lenin and "Gorky," but also confronts it more consciously. Wright describes how his notion of Bigger corresponded neither to the desires of moderate African-American leaders to display only positive images of Negro life to the white world, nor to the Communist Party's theoretical forecasts, in which African Americans played an exclusively positive role in revolutionary struggles. Wright dismisses the potential objections of the moderates, whom he feels live in a fantasy world where positive images can change material reality. However, he is more circumspect in the case of the potential Communist objections to Bigger. Wright is still a Party member, and he still grants the superiority of the Party's overall analysis of society and its stated goals. He nevertheless believes that the Bigger Thomases of the world are so thoroughly excluded from the economy, and thus so alienated from society—even from the society of the organized *opponents* of capitalism and racism—that there may be no place for them in the Marxist movement. This is the philosophical problem that compounds Wright's growing political incompatibility with communism.

Wright was aware of the Marxist analysis of that strata of the population, black and white, that lies even below the category of exploited laborers. He indicates his awareness by his discussion of Hitler and fascism. When Hitler came to power in Germany in 1933, his party had gained the allegiance of millions of the chronically unemployed, or lumpenproletarians. These hopeless and entirely alienated people were less susceptible to the positive philosophies of the socialist and communist parties, which were mainly embraced by the millions of organized workers. Insofar as the Nazis espoused a political philosophy, it was negative and incoherent, filled with hysterical rants against Jews, Bolsheviks, and "capitalist plutocrats." However, Hitler's mystical, anti-rational vision of the rebirth of the German nation, of a strong and prosperous "thousand-year Reich," appealed to these dispossessed millions, who had been ruined by the awful economic depression in Germany— a far worse depression than had been visited on the American economy. From a Marxist perspective, the organized working class has a duty to forge links with the unemployed, to organize their hunger marches and rent strikes, so that their sympathies would come to be with the workers, and not be easy prey for fascist demagoguery.

Wright was dissatisfied, however, with the Communist Party's attitude toward the unemployed ghetto-dweller. He also felt that the message of German nationalism—Nazism—had an African-American corollary in the philosophy of Marcus Garvey. Wright himself had rejected Garvey, whose "Universal Negro Improvement Association" sought ultimately to establish separate nations for

African Americans, preferably in Africa. The message of Garveyism, and black nationalism in general, has undeniable appeal for a minority people who have been as outraged as the descendents of Africans have been in America. Even the Communist Party recognized the seemingly implacable ferocity of American racism, at least in the South, and for a time proposed a "Black Belt State" for Negroes there. Wright felt that the simplistic message of Garveyism was potentially more appealing than Marxism to those African Americans who had found no place at all in American society. Let us recall that in *Native Son*, Wright makes Bigger express vague admiration for Hitler and Mussolini, and hope that "some day there would be a black man who would whip the black people into a tight band and together they would act and end fear and shame." At the same time, Bigger seems to enjoy laying the blame for Mary Dalton's death on Jan, the Communist. Bigger's sympathies are quite misplaced. Indeed, what could be more misplaced than an African-American's admiration for Hitler, the most diabolical racist murderer in history and a man who preached that blacks were not human beings, but monkeys? Wright tells us that he "tried to approach Bigger's snarled and confused nationalist feelings with conscious and informed ones of my own."

Wright's overall analysis of American society at this time is clearly Marxist. In 1940, when the depression was still convulsing the American economy, the potential existed for the victims of the convulsions to turn to either communism or to some form of hysterical nationalism. In the case of ruined white shopkeepers and chronically unemployed white workers, this second choice was fascism. In addition to the Ku Klux Klan, other American fascist movements were active during the Depression, including the Silver Shirts, Father Coughlin's National Union for Social Justice, and the German-American Bund, which was openly allied to Hitler's Nazis. It is hardly necessary to point out that these fascist organizations preached vile and deadly forms of hatred against Jews, against Catholics (in the case of the Ku Klux Klan) and, above all, against African Americans. Obviously, for African Americans, fascism is never a possible form of political expression. In Wright's view, Garveyism, or some other form of black nationalism, was communism's competitor for the sympathies of African Americans.

The question that Wright was considering was whether Bigger Thomas would "follow some gaudy, hysterical leader who'll promise rashly to fill the void in him, or whether he'll come to an understanding with the millions of his kindred fellow workers under trade-union or revolutionary guidance...." For Wright, the second alternative, Marxism, was the healthy course, but the success of that alternative depended upon a variety of factors. The more important factor, in Wright's words, was "the future drift of events in America." Marxists would call this factor the "objective" aspect of history. However, also of importance was the ability of the Communist Party—the "subjective" factor—to reach out adequately to African Americans, an ability about which Wright had his doubts.

One of Wright's objectives in writing *Native Son*, then, was to reveal truths about African-American life that were not understood, in his eyes, by his comrades in the Communist Party. If, he reasoned, Communists were to find their way to the Bigger Thomases, they must be made to see just how alienated they were even from the mainstream of organized labor opposition to the capitalist order. Yet Wright also approached what he believed was an aspect of alienation that was not susceptible to political analysis. As Wright relates in his lecture,

> There seems to hover somewhere in that dark part of all our lives, in some more than in others, an objectless, timeless, spaceless element of primal fear and dread, stemming, perhaps, from our birth (depending upon whether one's outlook upon personality is Freudian or non-Freudian!), a fear and dread which exercises an impelling influence upon our lives all out of proportion to its obscurity. And, accompanying this *first fear*, is, for the want of a better name, a reflex urge toward ecstacy, complete submission, and trust. The springs of religion are here, and also the origins of rebellion. In a boy like Bigger, young, unschooled, whose subjective life was clothed in the tattered rags of American "culture," this primitive fear and ecstasy were naked, exposed, unprotected by religion or a framework of government or a scheme of society whose final faiths would gain his love and trust; unprotected by trade or profession, faith or belief; opened to every trivial blast of daily or hourly circumstance. (pp. 528–29)

What we have here is Wright's early foray into psychological causation, and the philosophy of existentialism. He is saying that there are certain inherent aspects to Bigger's predicament and actions, not determined by social factors such as racism, poverty, or capitalism. In the political philosophy of black nationalism, all the principal forms of alienation suffered by African Americans are a product of racist society in which whites in general oppress blacks. To overcome alienation and oppression, blacks must separate from whites and form an exclusively black society. Marxism proposes a more generalized theory of alienation, wherein class oppresses class. Thus, both white and black workers are oppressed by a class of wealthy capitalists. Marxism does grant that African Americans are doubly oppressed—as workers, and as African Americans, but the way to freedom, to overcoming oppression, is to struggle in common with workers of all nationalities, to overthrow the capitalist order. The philosophical view that Wright hints at in the above-quoted passage, however, promotes the most generalized theory of alienation of all. In this psychological interpretation of suffering, everyone harbors a "primal fear and dread" inherently, as part of the human condition. There is no way to overcome it by struggling against an unjust society, because its causes are locked within the human mind itself.

This attitude is consistent with the philosophy of existentialism, which would not emerge by name until later in the 1940s. Insofar as he injected the theme of original estrangement into *Native Son*, Wright was an early existentialist. In fact, in a few years time, Wright would became politically and philosophically allied with Jean Paul Sartre, the most famous of all existentialist philosophers. Sartre was also an ex-communist who was repelled by Stalinism. While he did attempt to retain Marxist elements in his thinking, Sartre separated from Marxism by calling human estrangement a prior and permanent condition, from which there is no escape (he even called his famous play *No Exit*). This notion appealed to Wright as well, and while it did not cause him to abandon his commitment to African-American struggles, it eventually did impinge upon the coherence of his changing political philosophy. The existential human being is terribly alone, after all. The feeling of dread might be reduced if the person existed under certain favorable material circumstances, or had adopted comforting religious or political beliefs, but it would still be there, gnawing inside. Wright tells us that for Bigger Thomas, however, the dread (and the accompanying animal urge for momentary pleasurable release) are unbridled by wealth or philosophy. Bigger is facing his condition of primordial estrangement directly, and the results, as we come to know, are explosive and catastrophic. It is repellent to think that Bigger could not, under any circumstances, have overcome his alienated condition, but the feeling of repulsion is itself a very existential feeling. It accompanies consciousness of one's own insurmountable estrangement.

In its essentials, the psychological/existentialist interpretation of Bigger Thomas contradicts the naturalist/Marxist analysis. Yet Wright found a place for each in *Native Son*. It is clear that in 1940, at least, Wright believed that Marxism addressed the principal problems of human social organization under capitalism—hunger, homelessness, unemployment, racism, the oppression of women, and so forth. However, he also believed that once these problems were resolved in a socialist society, there would remain problems that issue from individual rather than social existence. By its introduction of the question of individual existence, Wright's novel cannot be classified simply as fine example of late literary naturalism. *Native Son* rather attempts to comprehend man as a social animal, and as the possessor of an irreducible individual existence. It is not a unique philosophic problem, but it is the most powerful one, and it would remain with Richard Wright, unresolved, all his life.

Sample Analytical Paper Topics

The following paper topics are designed to encourage your understanding of the novel as a whole, and to help you analyze important themes and literary techniques. A sample outline is included with each topic, indicating one (but not the only) possible approach to it.

Topic #1

Alienation is a very important theme in Richard Wright's novel. It is a concept that is also important in both Marxism and existentialism, two philosophies which Wright adopted and advocated during different periods in his life. One definition of alienation is that it is the condition in which all human beings are the creators of the wealth and culture of a society, but few are allowed to participate in the fruit of their creation. The majority are denied that enjoyment. Instead of controlling society, they are controlled by it. Instead of being or feeling included, they are excluded, or alienated. Discuss how Bigger's life is a life alienated from American society.

Outline

I.   Thesis Statement: *The title of the novel,* Native Son, *refers to Bigger Thomas, and suggests that he is a native of the United States, that he belongs here. Yet Bigger's experience is one in which he is everywhere denied his birthright and alienated from the society into which he has been born.*

II.   The conditions of Bigger's life

A.   Early life of poverty in segregated South.

B.   Family fled north after father was killed.

C.   In the North, he lives on welfare in one rat-infested tenement room with mother, brother, and sister.

D.   Faces choice of a life of petty crime, or one of menial labor as a servant.

III. Institutionalized racism in the 1930s America

A.   Segregated housing in North and South.

B.   African Americans excluded from serving on juries, and from specialized training, such as would be required for Bigger to have become an aviator.

C.   In the armed forces, African Americans confined to menial jobs.

IV.   Bigger's consciousness of his alienated condition

A.   Sees an airplane and tells his friend "I could fly one of them things if I had a chance."

B.   Views newsreel of Mary Dalton in Florida, having a "vacation," something he cannot have.

C.   "Sees" his rat-infested tenement room as if for the first time, after seeing how the Daltons live.

D.   States, in his first conversation with Max, that whites "own everything. They choke you off the face of the earth. They like God....They don't even let you feel what you want to feel. They after you so hot and hard you can only feel what they doing to you. They kill you before you die."

Topic #2

Throughout the novel, Richard Wright uses blindness as a metaphor for unconsciousness and ignorance, and sight as a metaphor for consciousness and understanding. With examples from the text, illustrate Wright's literary technique, and discuss Bigger's development within the context of blindness and sight.

Outline

I. Thesis Statement: *Literal and metaphorical references to "blindness" and "sight" abound in* Native Son, *and they give good indication of the relative consciousness or unconsciousness of many of the characters—especially Bigger—at any given point in time.*

II. Examples of blindness and sight

    A. Mrs. Dalton, who is literally *and* metaphorically blind, is herself a metaphor for the blind white power structure.

    B. Bessie Mears' transformation from self-admitted blindness to sight.

    C. Jan Erlone's transformation, which he conveys to Bigger in their meeting in Bigger's cell.

    D. Universal overview (absolute sight) in Boris Max's speech.

III. Bigger's blindness and sight

    A. Bigger's remarks to his friends about blacks and whites, and his frustation with his own lack of opportunity, indicate that he has sight early on.

    B. The sense of power Bigger derives from killing momentarily heightens his sight: he "sees" Bessie's blindness, and the blindness of his poor sister. He also "sees" his home as if for the first time.

    C. Bigger's blindness returns as his power diminishes, as he is pursued and caught.

    D. Return of Bigger's sight is indicated by his renewed interest in his own case, by his will to live, and especially by his brief relationship with Boris Max. He reveals his own true consciousness to another person for the first time, and he describes with great clarity what his life has been like.

    E. Limit on Bigger's development, and on Max's absolute sight, is Bigger's impending execution. Max is unable to communicate well, and Bigger arrives at an unsettling attitude toward his crimes. Bigger's attitude is understandable, given the life he has led, but it is a form of blindness, nonetheless.

Topic #3

Philosophers have long argued about how much *freedom* people have to decide their own actions, and to what degree their choices are made of necessity—influenced by forces beyond their control. Morality, the system whereby a person's action is judged to be good or bad, is dependent upon this issue of freedom of choice. If every person is equally and absolutely free to do whatever they want, then morality too may be equal and absolute, and everyone's actions can be judged according to the same standards. If, however, some people are more and others less free, then a more complex moral code may be needed. How much freedom does Bigger have to decide his own actions? Should his crimes be judged according to an absolute moral code?

Outline

I.   Thesis Statement: *At Bigger's trial, the author provides the reader with two conflicting moral codes. One is simple and absolute. It is voiced by David Buckley, Bigger's prosecutor, and holds that Bigger has committed monstrous crimes against society, that he is irredeemably evil and must be put to death. Bigger's lawyer, Boris Max, offers an opposing and more complex judgment of Bigger's actions, and one that is much more in keeping with the truth behind his crimes.*

II. Contradictions within Buckley's absolute morality

   A.   Fraught with racist terminology.

   B.   Based partly on a crime—the rape of Mary Dalton—that Bigger did not commit.

   C.   Assigns less importance to crimes against Bessie Mears than to those against Mary Dalton.

   D.   Makes his uncompromising judgment against Bigger partly for cynical reasons—to aid his own reelection campaign.

   E.   Treats other murderers, such as gangsters, with more leniency than Bigger.

III. Elements of Boris Max's view of morality

    A. Attempts to explain Bigger's actions and to seek their cause, rather than merely condemning them.

    B. States that Bigger's life has been defined by poverty, segregation, and servitude, conditions that have fostered fear and anger inside him.

    C. States that these conditions have been imposed upon Bigger and millions of other African Americans by a white power structure. Therefore African Americans—Bigger included—have not freely chosen the kind of lives they lead.

    D. States that Bigger killed Mary Dalton *inadvertently*, while attempting to keep from being discovered in a position that the white authorities have declared warrants the death penalty.

    E. States that Bigger's actions, including his terrible crimes, have therefore been largely determined by conditions imposed upon him by outside forces he does not control. The element of free choice in his actions has been negligible.

    F. Finally, states that Bigger must not, therefore, be executed as an evil criminal, because his crimes were an outgrowth of the only life he ever knew—a life of brutality and deprivation. Instead, he should go to prison, which would, ironically, be the best home he has ever known. Furthermore, as incredible as it may sound, as a prisoner he would have his first recognized relationship with official society.

Topic #4

The author's main purpose in *Native Son* was to portray in the starkest and most undeniably clear light, the separate and degraded existence of millions of African Americans, and to demonstrate how this existence is forced upon them, in specific ways by a specific power structure. It has been many decades since *Native Son* first appeared. To what extent have the conditions of African American life changed since the late 1930s, when Bigger Thomas and his family lived in the Depression-era Chicago ghetto?

Outline

I.   Thesis Statement: *While there have been many changes in African American life in the decades since the 1930s, the fundamental problems of poverty and racial segregation Richard Wright described in* Native Son *are still with us.*

II. Changes in African American life since the 1930s

    A.   Military desegregated after the Second World War.

    B.   Civil Rights movement won many rights and dismantled legal segregation in the South, through mass struggle in the 1950s and early 1960s.

        1.   Legal segregation of Southern schools ended.

        2.   Legal segregation in the South of public transportation, restaurants, bathrooms, ended.

        3.   Voting rights won in the South.

    C.   Struggles in the North won many legal rights, such as anti-discrimination laws in housing and employment.

III. What has remained unchanged since the 1930s.

    A.   Poverty, relative to white population.

    B.   *De facto* (actual) as opposed to *de jure* (legal) segregation in housing and schools: Bigger Thomas would easily recognize Chicago today, where the South Side ghetto is just as vast, as poor, and as black as it was in the 1930s.

    C.   Partial or total legal reversals of many of the gains made by working people over the years (such as affirmative action in hiring, the right to strike, and unemployment and welfare benefits) are today being contemplated by powerful politicians.

    D.   Principal reason Wright wrote *Native Son* was to expose racism and poverty in the North, where there was little, if any, legal segregation in the 1930s. The Northern political and economic power structure that Wright was criticizing remains in control of the country.

SECTION FIVE

Bibliography

Primary Sources

Fabre, Michel, and Charles T. Davis. *Richard Wright: A Primary Bibliography*. Boston: G.K. Hall and Co., 1982.

Kinnamon, Keneth (with the help of Joseph Benson, Michel Fabre, and Craig Werner).*A Richard Wright Bibliography: Fifty Years of Criticism and Commentary, 1933-1982*. Westport, Conn.: Greenwood Press, 1988.

Wright, Richard. *Native Son and "How 'Bigger' was Born"*. New York: HarperPerennial, 1993.

Secondary Works

Abcarian, Richard, ed. *Richard Wright's "Native Son": A Critical Handbook*. Belmont, Calif.: Wadsworth Publishing Co., 1973.

Brignano, Russell Carl. *Richard Wright: An Introduction to the Man and His Works*. Pittsburgh: University of Pittsburgh Press, 1970.

Butler, Robert. *Native Son: The Emergence of a New Black Hero*. Twayne's Masterwork Studies, No. 77. Boston: Twayne Publishers, A Division of G. K. Hall & Co, 1991.

Fabre, Michel. *The Unfinished Quest of Richard Wright*. Translated from the French by Isabel Barzun. Second edition. Urbana and Chicago: University of Illinois Press, 1993.

Gates, Henry Louis, Jr., and K. A. Appiah, eds. *Richard Wright: Critical Perspectives Past and Present*. New York: Amistad, 1993.

Gayle, Addison. *Richard Wright: Ordeal of a Native Son*. Garden City, New York: Anchor Press/Doubleday, 1980.

Kinnamon, Keneth. *The Emergence of Richard Wright: A Study of Literature and Society*. Urbana: University of Illinois Press, 1972.

Kinnamon, Keneth. Introduction to *New Essays on "Native Son"*. Edited by Keneth Kinnamon. Cambridge and New York: Cambridge University Press, 1990.

Reilly, John, ed. *Richard Wright: The Critical Reception*. New York: Burt Franklin, 1978.

Walker, Margaret. *Richard Wright: Daemonic Genius. A Portrait of the Man and a Critical Look at His Work*. New York: Amistad, 1988.

Webb, Constance. *Richard Wright: A Biography*. New York: G.P. Putnam's Sons, 1968.

MAXnotes®

REA's Literature Study Guides

MAXnotes® are student-friendly. They offer a fresh look at masterpieces of literature, presented in a lively and interesting fashion. **MAXnotes®** offer the essentials of what you should know about the work, including outlines, explanations and discussions of the plot, character lists, analyses, and historical context. **MAXnotes®** are designed to help you think independently about literary works by raising various issues and thought-provoking ideas and questions. Written by literary experts who currently teach the subject, **MAXnotes®** enhance your understanding and enjoyment of the work.

Available **MAXnotes®** include the following:

Absalom, Absalom!
The Aeneid of Virgil
Animal Farm
Antony and Cleopatra
As I Lay Dying
As You Like It
The Autobiography of
    Malcolm X
The Awakening
Beloved
Beowulf
Billy Budd
The Bluest Eye, A Novel
Brave New World
The Canterbury Tales
The Catcher in the Rye
The Color Purple
The Crucible
Death in Venice
Death of a Salesman
The Divine Comedy I: Inferno
Dubliners
Emma
Euripedes' Electra & Medea
Frankenstein
Gone with the Wind
The Grapes of Wrath
Great Expectations
The Great Gatsby
Gulliver's Travels
Hamlet
Hard Times

Heart of Darkness
Henry IV, Part I
Henry V
The House on Mango Street
Huckleberry Finn
I Know Why the Caged
    Bird Sings
The Iliad
Invisible Man
Jane Eyre
Jazz
The Joy Luck Club
Jude the Obscure
Julius Caesar
King Lear
Les Misérables
Lord of the Flies
Macbeth
The Merchant of Venice
The Metamorphoses of Ovid
The Metamorphosis
Middlemarch
A Midsummer Night's Dream
Moby-Dick
Moll Flanders
Mrs. Dalloway
Much Ado About Nothing
My Antonia
Native Son
1984
The Odyssey
Oedipus Trilogy

Of Mice and Men
On the Road
Othello
Paradise Lost
A Passage to India
Plato's Republic
Portrait of a Lady
A Portrait of the Artist
    as a Young Man
Pride and Prejudice
A Raisin in the Sun
Richard II
Romeo and Juliet
The Scarlet Letter
Sir Gawain and the
    Green Knight
Slaughterhouse-Five
Song of Solomon
The Sound and the Fury
The Stranger
The Sun Also Rises
A Tale of Two Cities
Taming of the Shrew
The Tempest
Tess of the D'Urbervilles
Their Eyes Were Watching God
To Kill a Mockingbird
To the Lighthouse
Twelfth Night
Uncle Tom's Cabin
Waiting for Godot
Wuthering Heights

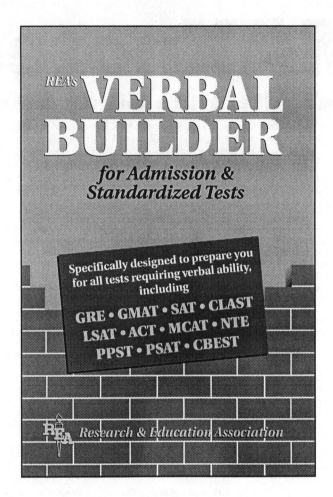

REA's **VERBAL BUILDER**

for Admission & Standardized Tests

Specifically designed to prepare you for all tests requiring verbal ability, including

GRE • GMAT • SAT • CLAST
LSAT • ACT • MCAT • NTE
PPST • PSAT • CBEST

Research & Education Association

Available at your local bookstore or order directly from us by sending in coupon below.